A COMPENDIUM OF
DECLINE AND DISTRUCTION
OF MAJOR CIVILIZATIONS
DURING ANCIENT TIMES

A COMPENDIUM OF DECLINE AND DISTRUCTION OF MAJOR CIVILIZATIONS DURING ANCIENT TIMES

Walter Whittemore

iUniverse, Inc.
Bloomington

A Compendium of Decline and Distruction of Major Civilizations During Ancient Times

iUniverse books may be ordered through booksellers or by contacting:

iUniverse
1663 Liberty Drive
Bloomington, IN 47403
www.iuniverse.com
1-800-Authors (1-800-288-4677)

ISBN: 978-1-4759-8501-6 (sc)
ISBN: 978-1-4759-8502-3 (ebk)

Printed in the United States of America

iUniverse rev. date: 05/18/2013

DEDICATION

This book is dedicated to my five children, Carol, Jim, Steve, Barbara and Bette, and also my deceased wife Constance (Connie) and my present wife, Yvonne, who had been very patient and understanding, realizing that I was engrossed in doing research and writing for hours which took away time usually devoted to her and her interests.

ACKNOWLEDGEMENT

This author can't say enough about his daughter, Barbara Tueichi, who did all the typing and spent hours doing the retyping of the errors that were made in the original draft.

INTRODUCTION

There have been many misconceptions what world history involves. The most common view is that it encompasses only dates, timelines and events. However, this idea is entirely false for, its parameters include societal changes, human lives, governmental organizations, technology, medicinal advances, religion, and geography. Therefore, one has to conclude that world history is an ongoing process that is changing constantly due to the reaction of peoples, their occupations and conditions.

Just as societies change so do people in their manners, behavior and thinking. This constant change has a direct effect on the conditions of civilization and its outcome.

Taking these facts into consideration, this author went ahead to explore those factors which eventually brought about the decline and collapse of the aforementioned parameters.

This study entailed a comprehensive and intelligent survey of these conditions.

In order to reach a plausible conclusion, certain questions had to be answered to give light on the subject matter. These include the following:

1. Who or what caused the decline or collapse of these civilized countries?
2. What was the result of the destruction?
3. What was the impact on civilization and society in these countries?

4. What were the changes in their culture, politics, geography, technology, science, medicine, religion, if any?
5. What effect did it have on human life and its ramifications?

To discover the answers to these pertinent questions, it was expedient to delve into the historical background which led to all these changes.

Therefore, it was extremely necessary to inquire and write a brief but intensive summary of the conditions and elements which brought about the collapse.

With this in mind, a venture into historical records were undertaken which will, I'm sure, enlighten the reader in the concepts of world history which bring about change for better or worse in the lives of humankind.

In some cases, knowledge of these incidents was limited and, in others, a more detailed and exact information was given. However, these faults do not detract from the significance of acquiring the knowledge of their demise.

Because of the extent of the historical downfall of countries and cities, this abridgement of historical events was limited to just ancient civilizations.

For those who are not familiar with the abbreviations of B.C.E. and C.E., they mean Before Common Era and Common Era.

The chapters are written in a chronological order to promote some form of continuity which will assist the reader in understanding the various civilizations and their decline and destruction.

CONTENTS

EGYPTIAN EMPIRE

Egypt has been known as the first civilization of Africa beginning in 3000 B.C.E. along the banks of the River Nile. It was in the Nile Valley where people began to establish communities. The Nile River was a great place to create settlements. For here, the rich soil that was dumped along the banks of the river during its yearly overflow provide a constant period of production of food, water, transport, and communication.

This period of ancient Egypt was identified by many dynasties, massive tomb construction, the development of hieroglyphic writing, and a centralization system of government.

It was during this period that Egypt was divided into small kingdoms—Upper Egypt in the south and Lower Egypt in the north. Lower Egypt was located on the Nile Delta and Upper Egypt in the south below the Fayun in the Nile River Valley.

It was the first Egyptian king, Menes, who united these two territories in 3110 B.C.E. and found a central government at Memphis. He was able to rule Egypt for sixty-two years. He established the first dynasty of what would eventually number 13 dynasties which ruled ancient Egypt for nearly 3000 years until Alexander the Great captured Egypt in 332 B.C.E.

The central government of Egypt was well established and mighty in the 3rd Dynasty around 2700 B.C.E. The kings and queens at this time were looked upon as gods. From about 2400 B.C.E. the king was the god Osiris, the lord of the Underworld. Also, the king was identified with the sun god Re and was known as the "Son of Re."

The history of ancient Egypt has been divided into three time periods—The Old Kingdom from 2700-2200 B.C.E., the Middle Kingdom from 2200-1786 B.C.E., and the new Kingdom from 1600-945 B.C.E.

It was during the Old Kingdom that Egypt developed a strong national government. It was situated from the capital city of Memphis. At this time, each king was regarded as a theocrat, that is, he held both political and religious power.

Holding this power, they were able to direct public works. One such work was the famous Step Pyramid at Saqqara built by King Djoser (Zoser) about the year 2600 B.C.E. Another famous construction was the Pyramids at Giza under King Khufu. This pyramid was the last remaining Wonder of the Ancient World.

"During the Old Kingdom Egypt was divided into 42 districts, or nomes, each one ruled by a representative of the king."

Kings, at this time, were either strong or weak. They decided where their capital was to be located and also their government.

His palace was usually built where the capital existed. This was one of the weaknesses of the hereditary monarchy.

It was during the third dynasty, 2613 B.C.E., that the kings began to be buried in pyramids. Ancient Egyptians believed in life after death. They believed that their souls lived forever so, they devised a way of preserving dead bodies by embalming them. This process was known as mummification. At first only pharaohs were mummified, but the privilege was extended in 2300 B.C.E. to anyone who could afford it. The whole process of mummification took more than two months to complete. The mummy's internal organs were stored in four jars. These containers were adorned with the heads of the dead person or with the gods.

During the Middle Kingdom, 2200-1783 B.C.E., the kings' authority of Egypt failed and the rulers of the nomes (districts) began to become independent. This lack of the kings' authority resulted in a series of wars which lasted for two centuries between groups of families. Finally, the wars ended when Ammenemes took the throne (1991-62 B.C.E.).

The Middle kingdom was founded by him and this was accomplished by destroying the power of the nobles and securing Egyptian borders. He was able to bring a period of artistic and literary development to the empire in addition to prosperity. This peaceful and prosperous period, which lasted approximately 200 years, finally collapsed about 1785 B.C.E., when Egypt was invaded and conquered by the Hyksos from the north.

The New Kingdom was founded by Ahmose I in 1570 B.C.E. He was able to oust the Hyksos and began a period of expansion. He reorganized the government as a military state. The future kings began period of conquest—Palestine, Nubia, Syria and extended the empire as far as the Euphrates River in Mesopotamia.

It was under Amenophis III, about 1417-1379 B.C.E., that Egypt reached its glory, wealth, and power. In Luxor, he built some magnificent temples in honor of the God Amun. The empire during these kings was enormous. It extended from Libya in the west to Mesopotamia in the east and from Syria in the north to Nubia in the south. Because of the extent of the empire, and the lack of natural borders, its borders were vulnerable to attacks. This caused a continual campaign by the kings to protect its borders in order not to undermine the empire.

It was during the 14th century, 1330 B.C.E., that Akhenaten became king. It seems that religion engulfed his entire behavior. He went about and changed his court from the worship of the god Amun to that of Aten. His original name was Amenhotep and, because of his obsession with the god Aten, he had changed his name to Akhenaten. The priesthood, however, were diametrically opposed to this change because of their belief in the god Amun. Because of his involvement with this religious change, Akhenaten's empire was in a state of uncertainty.

The result of this change was that all the provinces conquered in Asia over the previous 200 years were completely gone. Fortunately, these were regained by two outstanding pharaohs, notably Seti I and Ramesses II. These accomplishments were made in the last period of Egyptian magnitude.

Ramesses II decided to make peace with the Hittites accepting the loss of much of the northern empire. He fathered more than 100 children and his reign lasted 67 years. His descendants quarreled over his throne when he passed away. The victor during these squabbles was the father of Ramesses III, Setnakht.

Ramesses III, who took over the empire, struggled to save it. The Sea Peoples, in the eight years of his reign, invaded.

"Scholars have accepted that the Sea Peoples were in fact a mixed group, including contingents from the Aegean Islands, the west coast of Asia Minor, Mycenaean Greece, and perhaps even Syria."

He had already fought a battle against the Libyans when the Sea Peoples arrived. Because of a surplus of population and insufficient food, the economy of the Sea Peoples was disrupted.

The Sea Peoples' fleet and army raked havoc among other peoples and left a trail of death and destruction wherever they went. Their victory over the Hittites was outstanding.

Egypt's victories over the Sea Peoples were regarded as key battles of the ancient world.

They resulted in the preservation of Egypt and its culture which was to influence the Romans and Greeks later on.

It was at this juncture in history that Egypt was in a state of decline and the notorious Assyrians emerged to expand their kingdom.

However, the beginning of the end of the Egyptian empire and the New Kingdom period can be focused on the reign of Ramesses III in 1100's B.C.E. when he lost several wars in Syria.

By 945 B.C.E., the Egyptian Empire was severely shaken so that the Libyans from the south and the Kushites from the north were able to conquer this vast territory bringing a glorious close to a great empire.

Egypt, nevertheless, will always be remembered for its magnificent temples, its 365-day calendar which was used to track the stars for religious purposes, and also, for the flooding of the Nile. It was due to their skills in mathematics and engineering that the marvelous pyramids were built to house the dead bodies of the pharaohs. Their detailed study of anatomy of the human body was outstanding and was used in future generations for study and analysis.

Of course it goes without saying, the most prevalent achievement of the Egyptians was the mummification of the dead which gave archeologists an opportunity to gain an understanding of their culture by studying the artifacts which were recovered in their tombs.

The Western and the civilized world can be grateful to a great empire that contributed so much to posterity.

CHINESE EMPIRE

The history of the Chinese Empire is very fascinating as it encompasses one of intrigue, expansion, cruelty, leadership, despotism, technology, religion, and authority which was prosecuted under various dynasties.

Records have shown that it originated about 481 B.C.E., a period when the various feudal states were at war with one another ("Warring States Period") vying for control and supremacy. At the time, the emperors of the Eastern Zhou Dynasty had control but little authority over these states. By 280 B.C.E., these warring states were drawing toward a resolution and only six main kingdoms survived as independent states—Qin, Zhao, Wei, Han, Chu, and Zhou.

Of these states, the Qin emerged as the greatest defeating its main rival, the Zhou. Later on, he was able to subjugate the rest of these states.

In 312 B.C.E. the Qin dynasty was able to conquer the Ba and Shu kingdoms of northern Sichuan and parts of the Han Kingdom to the east.

In the year 221 B.C.E., Yeng Sheng who later conferred on himself the title of Huangdi, or emperor of a unified China (later called Shihuangdi by historians after his death), became emperor of the Qin dynasty. In 221 B.C.E., Qin conquered the remnants of the Zhou dynasty.

Shihuangdi was born in 258 B.C.E., the son of Xiao Wen, the ruler of Qin. At the age of 12 he took over the reins of government. In 221 B.C.E. he had formalized the unification of all the former kingdoms into a single magnificent state. He, then, went on to conceive a program which entailed a tremendous amount of nation building.

First, he disarmed the local warlords who had ruled independently for quite some time and subjected them to his rule. Second, because of the extent of his empire, he went ahead and divided his realm into 36 provinces govern by officials who were responsible of corresponding their transactions to him. Third, he began a series of new roads and canals which enviably improved communication throughout his realm. Fourth, he standardized weights and measures across China in order to improve trade. He even went to the extent to standardize the width of wagon axles, so all carts could run along the same road ruts (quite a conservative and less expensive idea to say the least).

By instigating these reforms, he was able to place his administration under his direct control. His government officials who resisted these reforms were put to work or put to death. Many were sent to the northern parts of the realm to help begin the Great Wall of China which he wanted to be built to protect his border from invaders, especially, the nomadic Mongols.

Most of the Qin wall is north of the Great Wall. The Ming dynasty is credited with constructing most of the Great Wall.

It is interesting to note that this colossal construction was only breached twice. Once during the reign of Kublai Khan (the Great Khan) who established the Yuan dynasty.

Despite these enormous accomplishments, Shihuangdi has been looked upon as an authoritarian despot. A black mark has been given to his reign.

Because of his refusal to accept the doctrine of Confucius, fearing the disruptive effect of his philosophical arguments on his united kingdom, Shihuangdi had his books burned at public ceremonies, and also, to his discredit, had some 400 dissident scholars killed. Yet, tyrant that he was, he was instrumental in forging a great nation into being. Without his efforts, imperial China would never have survived as it did for over 2,000 years.

Unfortunately, he died in the year 210 B.C.E., and again, civil war broke out among his heirs.

A rebel peasant, by the name of Liu Bang, massacred the entire Qin royal family and established the Han dynasty becoming its first emperor under the name of Gaozu.

The Han dynasty, nevertheless, continued the administrative system organized by Shihuangdi. The reforms in government and law that Shihuangdi had developed were not abolished during the Han reign. Han emperors had dissolved the philosophy of Confucius and in its place, the Legalist had gained notoriety. However, soon after the Qin demise, Confucianism became the official state philosophy. Also, the harsh laws of the Qin dynasty were moderated.

The end result of all this moderation was that the cultural and political unification and centralization of the Qin Empire continued under the Han Dynasty which went on to establish the Mandarin social and political system which survived as the basis of Chinese society and included the Ch'ing (Manchu) Dynasty.

The Qin dynasty will be forever remembered for all its accomplishments beside its political and military unity.

Shihuangdi, emperor of the Qin dynasty feats include: a unified set of weights and measures throughout the empire, standardized coinage, various implements, especially, the axle length of wagons in order to avoid variation so that the carts could cover the same ruts as the previous ones, construction of roads and canals, a system unified laws for the entire empire, and the standardization of the written language.

The classical period of China was deluged with a whole host of advancements in technology and science. These included, in the field of astronomy, the calculation of the solar year as 365 ¼ days, and also, predicted eclipses of the sun and moon. Even Halley's Comet in 240 B.C.E. was predicted.

In agriculture, an irrigation system was improved. Crops were fertilized with human waste and livestock was attended to by medicine.

Key inventions included the wheelbarrows, compass, gunpowder, paper, and suspension bridges.

All these advancements and achievements brought peace and prosperity to China and certainly improved the living conditions of the populace and made life more pleasant and easier.

Two major accomplishments have to be noted. First, the Silk Road was constructed by the emperor Han Wu-Ti about 100 B.C.E. which was used for trade between Europe and China. This road was 3,728 miles long which connected the Mediterranean to Asia which consisted of a series of routes. Products, such as Chinese silk, gunpowder, spices, gold, metals, clocks, coins, jewelry, and glass travelled along this famous road.

Second, over 2,000 years after Qin died in 1974, his burial tomb was discovered untouched by grave robbers. His burial grounds were located near the city of Xian in central China. Legend has it that it took 700,000 prisoners who labored for years to build this extraordinary earthwork.

Here, in wood-roofed vaults, stands an army of life-size terracotta figures of 7,000 generals, officers and soldiers with spears to guard as bodyguards in the afterlife of the emperor. It has been said that no two faces are alike.

Finally, the conquest of northern China, after Genghis Khan's death, was left to his grandson, Kublai Khan who became emperor of China in 1259. After 19 years, Kublai established the Yuan dynasty which was to last more than 100 years until a rebellion drove this dynasty from the throne.

Thus, a great magnificent empire came to a reputable conclusion but, its achievements are still recognized today throughout the world.

SUMERIAN EMPIRE

Little is known of the origins of the Sumerians but it is surmised that they migrated from an area close to the Caspian Sea which is located between Europe and Asia and is the "largest inland body of water in the world."

They entered Mesopotamia (Iraq) at an early age, around 5500 B.C.E., and were the first people to erect the first cities. They were the first people to record history and develop an hereditary kingship. Most of all, they were the first people to create an urban civilization.

Because of Sumer's location near the rivers of Tigris and Euphrates which occasionally overflow each year, they had to build flood walls, canals and reservoirs. The flooding of the land caused fertile farmland which in turn created crop production on a large scale. These people were very inventive because they had to innovate technology to produce the crops of barley, linseed and wheat.

The inventions which they created are the arch, sundial, twelve month calendar, wagon wheel, sailboat, potter's wheel, metal plow and a number system based on 60. Their development of math grew out of the need for record-keeping in trade and mainly in administration. We use this system based on 60 in telling our time today.

Because of these innovations, a steady increase in the production of crops was realized. The effect was an increase in population and the growth of cities. People left their farms and migrated to the cities. Sumerians became merchants and traders while others became skilled craftsmen and religious and political leaders. This influx of migration created city-states governed by a council of elders.

When threatened by outside peoples, these elders were forced to appoint a military commander called a <u>lugal</u> ("great man"). Eventually they assumed permanent power and their title came to mean "king." This position was hereditary.

By 3000 B.C.E. the Sumerians had created 12 city-states which had independent rule. A massive stone structure called the ziggurat was placed in the center of the city. A temple was erected on the top of this structure which was dedicated to the god each city-state worshipped. These gods ruled the activities of humans and also the forces of nature. Eventually, the city-state developed a monarchy of leadership. The kings also assumed the position of high priest to the city-state god. This connection of priest and king was instrumental in the development of a stable city-state.

This stability enabled the people to achieve impressive new-developments. One such achievement was the first form of writing called <u>cuneiform</u>. This involved the wedge-shaped marks on wet clay tablets by using a reed. Because of this new development, a whole host of scribes emerged who kept records of various transactions, historical developments and writings about myths.

After a time, pictures were placed on clay which represented words or sounds. These were "written in a straight line rather than a column and were read from left to right."

From around 2275 B.C.E., Sargon I, king of Akkad, north of Sumer, built an empire from Syria to the Persian Gulf. Because of the expansion of his domain, he was able to unite all the Sumerian cities under his control.

Sargon was a sheepherder's son. His name means "the king is just." He was a fruit grower and later became a cupbearer to a local ruler before becoming the king of Akkad, a city in Mesopotamia. This city became prosperous because of its trade and to protect its trade routes he conquered lands and prevented other rulers from charging tolls. Merchants sailed to the Persian Gulf in their trading transactions. The Mesopotamian cities, of Lagash and Ur, from time to time, were forced to fight other cities, such as, Umma for water and land rights. These cities were also in constant warfare with the nomads of the Arabian Desert and nearby mountain peoples.

Sargon, in order to protect his empire, had to organize a large army to ward off his enemies.

Not satisfied with his power as king, he set out to conquer other city-states of Mesopotamia. He was victorious in most of his campaigns except he was unable to conquer the city-state of Ebla. His Akkadian Empire crumbled soon after his death due to the defense and bullishness of this city-state. Due to a counterattack, Ebla was able to gain possession of the entire Fertile Crescent.

Ebla's possession of this enormous piece of land didn't last. This fertile land was too valuable to become unnoticed and other regimes tried to possess this valuable piece of property.

By the year 2000 B.C.E., a tribe of Amorites from west Syria got greedy and conquered the city-state of Ebla. It didn't take long before the rest of the kingdom fell into their hands including the great city of Babylon which became the capital city for their new empire.

Thus, a great empire came to a horrific close due to warfare and greed of their neighbor, the Amorites, who wanted to extend their empire and gain a powerful position in the Fertile Crescent.

The Amorites continued their expansion across the Fertile Crescent and finally gobbled up the famous city of Babylon noted for its Hanging Gardens which became their capital city.

The end result of this disaster was a dissemination and a meshing of the Sumerian people, loss of their culture and land to their conquerors, and most important of all, their magnificent empire.

INDIA EMPIRE

The civilization in the Indus Valley in northwestern India goes back a long way. It has been recorded to have been established about 4500 B.C.E. Its two chief cities at this time were Harappa and Mohenjo-Daro.

It is amazing to note that these people possessed streets planned on a grid-system and had drainage systems. They also possessed temples, baths, and magnificent public buildings and private homes.

In addition, they used a system of weights and measures.

Then, suddenly, it seems that all this fortune came to an abrupt end and its civilization ceased.

One reason for this collapse has been blamed on the flooding of the Indus River. Also, because of the over-use of the local forests, an environmental disaster resulted.

Archeologists have discovered centuries later that the warlike Aryans from central Asia arrived about 1500 B.C.E. and raised havoc by burning villages and cities and slaughtering its people.

By 500 B.C.E., the Indian subcontinent was a land of petty kingdoms and some of these acquired great wealth. These cities were located in the Indus River valley and the Ganges.

It was during the next millennium that two great empires emerged—the Gupta and Mauryan. Credit for spreading the Buddhist faith goes to the Mauryan rulers, whereas, the Guptas engaged in the revival of Hinduism.

At the close of the Vedic Age, King Bimbisara from 542 to 495 B.C.E., was able to expand the kingdom of Magadha and consolidate his power through conquest and marriage. This resulted in India's first true empire.

Then, in 321 B.C.E. Chandragupta Maurya seized the kingdom of Magadha and found the Mauryan Empire. Later, he gave the throne to his son Bindusara in 300 B.C.E. who extended the Maurya rule into India's Deep South.

Bindusara's son, Asoka took over the realm in 269 B.C.E. and who was probably the most important king in the history of India. He was the grandson of Chandragupta Maurya the founder the Maurya dynasty.

Chandragupta was a military leader who conquered most of northern India.

The date of Asoka birth is unknown—guess is around 300 B.C.E.

Around 269 B.C.E. Asoka ascended the throne. His first move was militarily. It was during the eight year of his reign that he launched a military attack against Kalinga, a state located on the east coast of India which turned out to be a successful campaign. This battle cost the lives of 100,000 men. Sickened by the violence and blood of his victory, he became very remorseful and decided that he would not engage in another battle to extend his empire any further in India. Because of this battle Asoka was converted to Buddhism and made it the state religion. He, also, renounced all warfare.

Under his rule a third of the six councils met to discuss the teachings of Buddha and the orders of Buddhism. However, the result was a failure in trying to unite the main differences between the various branches of the Buddhist faith.

Asoka was a very benevolent ruler. For instance, he tolerated other religions in his domain. He allowed Hinduism to be practiced in the empire. His orders and decrees were propagated in the entire country through inscriptions which were carved onto pillars throughout his realm.

Because of his interest and belief in Buddhism, he began to spread this religion through his missionaries (monks), into Sri Lanka, and also, into Central Asia where it emphasized the scholarly Mahayana tradition. These missions were especially successful in Ceylon.

Asoka's humane and political policies that he adopted should not go unnoticed. He established hospitals and sanctuaries for animals. He built roads and harsh laws were mitigated. His appointment of officials to serve in his government was to instruct people in the development of friendly human relations.

After his death in 232 B.C.E., the Mauryan Empire began to decline. The last Mauryan ruler was overthrown and the region dissolved into smaller kingdoms.

These kingdoms fought to gain political control and, while this was going on, India was invaded by various peoples, such as, the Sakas and the Kushans, nomads originally from China who arrived in India 100 B.C.E. The Kushans were assimilated into Indian society and eventually became the warrior class. Their most powerful ruler was Kanishka who was a convert to Buddhism. He organized a council of Buddhist monks who were delegated to regulate the teachings of Buddha.

The Gupta Empire was founded by Chandragupta I, a ruler from the Magadha kingdom, who was 'fed up' with outside rulers.

It was Chandragupta's son, Samudragupta, who conquered much of northern and eastern India, and thereby, bringing the Kushan Empire to an end.

However, it was under Chandragupta II who ruled from 376 to 415 C.E., that the empire reached the height of its power and influence. This period was noted as the Golden Age of India even though it lasted for about 200 years. During this short period of existence, the society of India thrived.

Hinduism was the official religion of the empire. It began to flourish because of the stability of the Empire. Many temples were built to honor the different sub-gods of the religion. The empire experienced a growth of learning because it gave to its people many freedoms.

Some of the achievements during this stage of stability were the creation of the concepts of algebra, the explanation of the concept of zero took place, and the numerals one through nine were recognized.

Hospitals were found and doctors were able to reset broken bones. Astronomy took a great leap as the astronomers knew that the world was round.

It was a time when prosperity was at its height. Trade expanded to all regions of the empire—China, central Asia, Arabia, and Rome.

As all good things have to come to an end so did India's Golden Age. Its wealth and prosperity attracted invaders, such as the White

Huns of Asia which weakened the government and its military due to its constant protection of its borders.

The Gupta Empire was broken up into many small kingdoms in 600 C.E. and they vied for control of the Indian subcontinent.

Nevertheless, this wasn't a complete collapse, as the culture of the Gupta Empire survived to influence India for future centuries.

As a final thought, Siddhartha Gautama should be mentioned because it was he, at the age of 29, who left his wife and family and wandered for seven years throughout India in the search for the meaning of suffering and of life. At the end of this wandering, he realized what the meaning of life consisted of and, he shared his enlightenment with a large gathering of people. It was during this time that his followers called him Buddha or the "Enlightened One."

Buddha taught that there were Four Noble Truths:

"First, all people suffer and know sorrow. Second, people suffer because of their desires. Third, they can end their suffering by eliminating these desires. Fourth, to eliminate those desires, people should follow the Buddha's Eightfold Path."

"The Eightfold Path consisted of knowing the truth, resisting evil, saying nothing to hurt others, respecting life, working for the good of others, freeing the mind from evil, controlling thoughts, and practicing meditation." By following the Eightfold Path, one could achieve nirvana (an ideal state, heaven or paradise) which involved a state of freedom from rebirth or the state of extinction.

Buddha traveled across India for 45 years teaching his philosophy of religion and converting thousands of followers.

Later, Buddhism split into two different sects. The Theravada sect which looks upon Buddha as a great teacher whose philosophy should be read. The other sect was the Mahayana who sees Buddha as a savior of the people and who believes he is a god. The religion of Buddha wasn't received very well in India. This could be because he rejected the caste system which dealt with inequalities, whereas, the ruling class and priests regarded it as a necessary means for survival.

Today, the religion of Hinduism is followed by a majority of Indians.

MINOAN EMPIRE

About the year 2000 B.C.E., the Minoan civilization emerged on the small island of Crete. Unfortunately, little is known about this civilization. Our knowledge about this civilization was due to an English archeologist named Sir Arthur Evans who discovered a famous palace at Knossos in 1894. He excavated the grounds there for several years and eventually found this colossal building with its hundreds of rooms.

This lavish building was constructed with stone and mud brick which was decorated in brightly colored frescoes.

This construction showed the amazing skill of the artists, architects, and engineers at this time.

The Minoan reputation had spread over the eastern Mediterranean. Over a period of 300 years, they produced fine metalwork in bronze and gold besides glittering pottery with its colored decorations. They, also, invented a form of writing called linear A which replaced their pictorial script but has not yet been deciphered.

The Minoans accumulated wealth by trade which extended across the eastern Mediterranean. Because of this increase in wealth, they were able to establish towns and ports and great palaces at Knossos, Phaestos, Mallia, and Zakro.

At Knossos, many artifacts were found. It had many courtyards and supplied workshops for its craftspeople and quarters for their lodging.

These energetic people constructed stone roads and bridges. They had aqueducts for carrying water and a drainage system.

They wove and dyed cloth. They cultivated the land which produced surplus crops which they exported and brought additional wealth to their economy. The royal family even had toilets and showers which is most extraordinary for this period of time.

All in all, these people enjoyed games, music, dance, and entertainment.

There is a Greek legend which is too fascinating to leave unnoticed or overlooked. That was about the "God Zeus who fell in love with a princess called Europa. According to legend, he turned into a white bull and swam to Crete with her on his back. They had three sons, one of whom was Minor, who became the king of Crete."

The bull was worshipped as a sacred animal and sports were organized in its behalf.

In this sport, the participant had to somersault over a bull's horns.

About 1450 B.C.E. a huge disaster took place in Crete. A volcano erupted on Mount Thera which created a huge tidal wave which engulfed the entire island. This disaster so weakened the island that the Mycenaeans were able to conquer it.

The Mycenaeans flourished from about 1650 B.C.E. to 1200 B.C.E. The Mycenaean civilization was destroyed in the 12th century after they defeated the city of Troy. The fighting between the two countries lasted for ten years. However, this period of conquest came to an abrupt end when the Dorians, a people from the northwestern part of the Greek mainland, took control of the Peloponnesus, the southern peninsula of Greece.

The overthrow of this civilization is known as the Dark Ages or Archaic Period which lasted from 1100 B.C.E. to about 800 B.C.E.

PERSIAN EMPIRE

One of the all time greats of ancient times was Cyrus the Great, who as a military leader had extended his empire from the Mediterranean Sea to the Indus River in India. Cyrus was the son of Cambyses, a Persian nobleman, and Mandane, the daughter of Astyages, king of Media. According to the writings of Herodotus, Greek historian from Athens, the legend has it that one day Cyrus would overthrow Astyages, king of the Medes. Astyages thought that he would defeat Cyrus in battle but, instead, the reverse took place and Cyrus overthrew Astyages and became ruler over the Medes.

Because the Medes and the Persians were closely linked, both in language and in origins, the change was regarded as a transformation of dynasties instead of a victorious conquest.

Cyrus retained much of the administrative apparatus of the Medes in addition to most of its laws.

Not satisfied with this conquest, his eyes centered on the Lydian Empire in Asia Minor ruled by King Croesus. By 546 B.C.E., Cyrus had conquered this empire and had taken Croesus, his prisoner.

Cyrus did not stop here for, in a series of campaigns, he subdued all of eastern Iran and utilized all its major contributions.

His next move was toward the wealthy Babylonian Empire located in central Mesopotamia which ruled the entire Fertile Crescent. Because Nabonidus, the Babylonian ruler was not in the best relationship with his subjects, when the armies of Cyrus advanced on the city in 539 B.C.E., the Babylonians surrendered without a fight. As a result of this conquest, Syria and Palestine which were under the rule of Persia were added to his domains.

After a period of rest in which he spent consolidating his rule, he led an army to the northeast to conquer the Massagetae who were a nomadic tribe living in Central Asia.

After winning the first bout against the fierce Scythian Massagetae, they were defeated in the second encounter in 529 B.C.E. and Cyrus was slain during the battle.

Cambyses II, the son of Cyrus, went on to defeat the Massagetae in another engagement and was able to recover his father's body which he buried at Pasargadae, the Old Persian capital.

After this engagement, Cambyses II conquered Egypt which united the entire ancient Middle East into a single empire.

Cyrus was not only a great military leader but had other traits of far greater proportion. He possessed a fine benign character. He was tolerant of other religions and people's customs.

He freed thousands of Hebrews who had been brought to Babylon as captives by King Nebuchadnezzar.

The Persian Empire crumbled in 333 B.C.E. at the Battle of Issus, when Alexander the Great, the Macedonian General, defeated Darius III of Persia.

Cyrus is not only noted for the expansion of his empire and his conquests in battle but, of greater importance is his establishment of an empire which "permanently altered the political structure of the ancient world."

BABYLONIAN EMPIRE

It is interesting to note, after the Amorites conquered Babylon, they had meshed with them and were then called Babylonians. These people absorbed much of the culture from the areas which they had conquered. They adopted the Sumerian language and, most important of all, their cuneiform writing which they used in transacting business operations, trade and other valuable pursuits. They also copied the Sumerian social structure which encompassed three classes of people in their society. The slaves were at the bottom of the heap. Next came what they called the middle class of merchants, artisans, and farmers. At the top of this social structure were the nobles, priests and most important of all, the kings who ruled with strict authority.

Their greatest achievements came under the rule of the powerful monarch, King Hammurabi. His first quest brought the entire Fertile Crescent under his command which included the lands of Sumer and Akkad.

He was the sixth of their ruling dynasty. He reigned between around 1790 B.C.E. and 1750 B.C.E.

He was a very capable administrator as shown in his innovation of his tax structure which made it much easier to collect revenue. These taxes were used in a beneficial manner which helped to increase the prosperity of his people by increasing the productivity of agriculture. To do this he was wise enough to repair the broken down irrigation canals in order to water and fertile the lands.

The high-light of his administration can be the code of laws which he assembled throughout the land which he unified to create one law code for the entire empire. These laws were carved on a huge stone slab and were discover by French archeologists in 1901.

"The Code consisted of 282 laws and another 35 were found to be chipped off and lost." The Code stipulated specific crimes and their penalties. For instance, if a surgeon caused the death of a man during an operation by using a knife, he in turn would lose his hand. One can see how strict these laws had been.

This Code extended beyond the legal code as it encompassed the structure of government and religious life because the king was regarded as the chief priest. The Code of laws were published for all the people to see even though it did not treat the classes of people equally.

This code of laws was the precursor of our modern day legal system which governs our societies today.

It was unfortunate that the decline of the Babylonian Empire came with the death of Hammurabi and eventually fell to the warlike Hittites in the 1600's B.C.E.

These people by 2000 B.C.E. had migrated to Mesopotamia from the area around the Black Sea and had dominated most of Asia Minor. They went on a rampage in 1595 B.C.E. and conquered the Babylonian Empire by using chariots and iron weapons.

They had launched their campaigns from their capital city at Hattusas. In 1200 B.C.E. their abrupt rule came to an end.

This famous empire collapsed because of the greed of the war-like Hittites whose thirst for land was over-whelming. One good thing survived from this onslaught and that was Hammurabi's legal code which today forms the basis of our legal system.

Other endeavors which are worth mentioning are the hanging Gardens of Babylon, one of the Seven Wonders of the Ancient World and the conquest of Judah in the 6th century B.C.E. The Jews had been exiled to Babylon and it was through the persuasion of the prophet Daniel, who became a counselor to the king, that they were allowed to return to their homeland. This event in Jewish history has been known as the Babylonian Captivity.

They shone in two other areas where they progressed—astronomy in which they were able to predict lunar eclipses by 1000B.C. and, in mathematics, where they calculated a circle of 360 degrees and the hour of sixty minutes. Their highlights were the development of mathematical tables and algebraic geometry. These developments have been used extensively at the present time in our schools and colleges.

ISRAELITE EMPIRE

The history of Israel and the Jews has been a long sad chaotic one of persecution and exile. The Jews, even up to the 19th century, were persecuted by anti-Semitic groups in Central and Eastern Europe which brought about a large number of immigrants to Palestine, especially from Russia. Because of the Balfour Declaration of 1917, hundreds of thousands of Jews settled in Palestine which caused Arab protests. Since then, the Palestinians and the Jews have had several disagreements which led to five wars in 45 years and the end doesn't seem in sight.

But these events are only one segment of the Jewish history. One has to go back into historical times to discover why and when all this turmoil and wars began. Most of the history of this civilization has emanated from archaeological records and the Bible.

Back in 1900 B.C.E., God appeared to Abraham on several occasions promising him and his people the land of Canaan.

Abraham, a great prophet, was born in the ancient city of Ur in Mesopotamia.

Tradition has it that Abraham's wife, Sarah, gave birth to Isaac. They were 100 years old at the time.

According to the Bible, God told Abraham to sacrifice his son. Just as he was about to commit this act, angels appeared and told him to stop.

This story has been interpreted in many ways. One, which is most likely, is that it was a precursor to the sacrifice of Jesus.

Abraham, the father of the nation of Israel, left Ur and settled in Canaan.

The Canaanites, who the Greeks know as Phoenicians, were a Semitic people whose empire consisted of Canaan, Syria, and part of Mesopotamia.

The Israelites became firmly ensconced in Canaan about 1130 B.C.E. They believed in a monotheistic deity and a strict code of ethics. They believed that God made a covenant or promise with Abraham that he would have Canaan 'a land of milk and honey.'

Abraham's son, Jacob, raised 12 sons who became the leaders of the 12 tribes of Israel.

Because of a drought in Canaan, the Israel tribes had to migrate to Egypt where they were enslaved.

Around 1250 B.C.E., after working as slaves in Egypt, the tribes under the leadership of Moses were allowed to leave.

The book of Exodus in the Bible gives an account of Moses leading his people through the desert for 40 years in search of the 'Promised Land,' the land of Canaan.

It was on Mount Sinai that God revealed to Moses the Ten Commandments which he carved into stone tablets. These Commandments were kept in a portable shrine, the Ark of the Covenant, during their stay in the desert.

Unfortunately, Moses wasn't given the privilege of entering Canaan but died on the outskirts of the land. The Israelites entered Canaan about 1000 B.C.E. where they ousted the Canaanites and the Philistines.

There are three major achievements given to Moses. "First, he has been given the credit for leading the Hebrews in the Exodus from Egypt. Second, he has been the reputed author of the first five books of the Bible, namely, Genesis, Exodus, Leviticus, Numbers, and Deuteronomy. The books constitute the Jewish Torah or Bible. These books include the Mosaic Code or laws which governed the conduct of the Jews in biblical times. The Code includes the Ten Commandments. Third, Moses has been given the honor of being the founder of Jewish monotheism. However, the Old Testament explicitly credits Abraham as the founder of monotheism."[1]

---

[1]   Hart, H. Michael. The 100 a Ranking of the Most Influential Persons in History. N.Y. Carl Publishing Group, 1995.

In 1020 B.C., Saul was selected as king by the tribes. He established the first kingdom in Israel after he defeated the Philistines and the Ammonites. He is credited for uniting the 12 tribes.

The Philistines continued to wage war even after their defeat. King Saul's three sons were killed in battle. Saul, who is thought to have suffered some form of mental depression, committed suicide.

David followed Saul as the king of Israel and made Jerusalem his capital. He, immediately, increased the function of the central government by reorganizing it. He, also, enlarged the kingdom of Israel.

David has been noted as Israel's greatest king. He was a shepherd and musician from Bethlehem at one time. His reputation was built on his allegorical defeat of the Philistine giant, Goliath. He was elected king of the Hebrews and united the various Jewish tribes. He made Jerusalem his capital after its capture. Since then it has been known as the city of David. It was here that the Ark of the Covenant was located.

Solomon, the son of David, took over the throne in 965 B.C.E. and between them they created an empire that extended from Elath on the Red Sea in the south into present-day Syria in the north.

An efficient bureaucracy enabled Solomon's kingdom to acquire the stability needed to strengthen it. In addition, a professional army was organized which included an élite corps of charioteers comprising 1,400 vehicles and 4,000 horses.

Israel witnessed an economic increase in productivity because of an extensive trade with Phoenician states and an explosive program of building. One such structure was the great Temple of Jerusalem on Mount Moriah which housed the Ark of the Covenant.

Solomon's fame knew no bounds as it spread far and wide. He has been known for his wisdom and the Queen of Sheba travelled some 1,500 miles to establish trade with Israel and witness the great wisdom of this magnificent king.

In order to pay for his building programs, especially, the magnificent temple in Jerusalem, he taxed his people and his son, Rehoboam, continued the father's same method of taxation. Resenting this burden, the northern tribes split away from the southern kingdom of Judah and formed a separate Jewish kingdom called Israeli in about 925 B.C.E. with its capital at Samaria.

The Assyrians, a Mesopotamian people from the Tigris Valley, developed siege engines and mail armor. With these innovations, they were able to capture Israel who, because of internal discord, was so weaken that they fell as easy prey in 721 B.C.E.

The southern Jewish kingdom of Judah survived the defeat and became a vassal of the great Babylonian Empire.

In 598 B.C.E., the people of Judah revolted against Babylonian rule. Nebuchadnezzar, the Babylonian king, crushed the uprising. Ten years later, the Jews of Judah revolted again. This time Nebuchadnezzar destroyed the city of Jerusalem and its temple and deported thousands of Jews to Babylon.

The Israelites were happy when Cyrus the Great, the Persian king, overthrew Babylon in 539 B.C.E. Because of his benevolence, they were allowed to return to their homeland which was part of his empire.

Many accepted the invitation to go home, although many preferred to stay in Babylon or in Egypt. This was the beginning of the dispersion or 'Diaspora' of the Jewish people that continued into modern times.

The hardship of the Jewish people didn't end here. Later, they were conquered by Alexander the Great and, still later, the Roman Empire.

The area once covered by Israel and Judah fell to Seleucius I Nicator, one of Alexander's generals. A rebellion broke loose led by the priest Judas Maccabaeus against Seleucid's attempts at Hellenisation which, in 165 B.C.E., resulted in the independence of Judah.

The Romans got involved in a dispute over the throne of Judah in 63 B.C.E. which, in a very short time, was added to its empire.

In 66 C.E., a huge rebellion led by the zealots took place which required a massive Roman army to quell it. The result was most alarming. The Temple was destroyed and captives were sent to Rome as slaves. In 70 C.E. hundreds were forced to leave the country.

This was called the 'Diaspora', the dispersion. Many of them decided to remain in Palestine and it did not officially end for nearly 19 centuries until the slaughter of Jews in the Holocaust during WWII. The outcome was the creation of the modern state of Israel by the United Nations in 1947.

OLMEC EMPIRE

It is interesting to note how many advanced civilizations occupied Central America or Mesoamerica during ancient times. Several have been recorded by historians and archeologists, namely the Olmecs, Nceyans, Toltecs, Aztecs, and the Teotihuacans.

In the year 1200 B.C.E., the Olmecs settled in east—central Mexico and were very industrious until 400 B.C.E. They were the first civilization to settle in America. They are best known for the huge heads which were carved from basalt with Chinese facial forms and which measured over three metric high. According to scholars, these heads probably represented their rulers. Some of these heads are adorned with helmets which suggest some form of a ballgame. The Olmecs did devise a ritual ballgame which was played on special courts.

Other Central American civilizations did adopt these ritual ballgames.

It is interesting to note that the players weren't allowed to touch the ball with their hands or feet. They had to use their elbows, thighs and hips to control the ball.

This set of rules immediately brings to one's mind the modern game of soccer which is very popular in Mexico and the South American countries today.

The Olmecs earned part of their living through trade with other countries across Central America and, in many instances, controlled huge amounts of trade.

This information concerning trade has been gathered from ornaments, sculptures, and artifacts which were found in northern Mexico, Costa Rica and El Salvador.

The Olmecs were highly skilled mathematicians and had developed a form of picture writing.

Their arithmetic consisted of a system of dots and bars. The dots represented the figure, and the bar, 5. A zero was represented by a shell. By using this unique system they were able to calculate complex problems.

About 1200 B.C.E., the villages linked with each other to form large settlements. These settlements contained ceremonial centers, large public buildings, shops and homes. Society was divided between peasant farmers who built the ceremonial centers and the wealthy ruling class. A small number of traders and craftsmen completed this social structure.

About the year 900 B.C.E., the peasants became angry on the demands laid on them by the ruling class and they destroyed the town of San Lorenzo which housed the monumental heads in the courts where they were defaced and destroyed.

Other centers were erected which took the place of San Lorenzo. One was La Venta located on an island in the Tonalá River. It, too, was overthrown. Tres Zapotes was the last to be overthrown by the rebellious peasants.

With its destruction in 200 B.C.E., the Olmec civilization came to an end.

Nevertheless, the Olmec influence did affect other cultures, such as, the Mayans, Toltecs, and the Aztecs.

Their legacy will be remembered in history because of their achievements in art, architecture, language, mathematics, and writing.

MAYAN EMPIRE

The Mayan civilization was established in the Yucatan peninsula, Guatemala, Belize, Honduras, and southern Mexico about 1000 B.C.E. This civilization has been called the ("Greeks of the New World"). They created a culture of such importance that it has sometimes been regarded as the greatest in all Mesoamerica. They prospered culturally and politically from about 250 to 950 C.E.

By 300 C.E., they recorded their history on large stone slabs by using hieroglyphics. The Mayans had a system of numbering like ours which they counted in twenties and in which the same symbol could stand for different values according to its position. This system consisted of bars and dots that made over 850 characters.

Their astronomers knew how to calculate the length of a year. They could predict solar eclipses and were able to chart the orbit of Venus.

The Mayan sculptors were very skilled. They made beautiful statues and carvings. They had brilliant architects who built beautiful cities such as Chichén, Itza, Uxmal, and Tikal. Their palaces were made of great slabs of stone which were covered with a layer of plaster. They were decorated with pictures of kings and gods. Their temples were built the same way and were painted with a bright red color. These temples were situated at the top of pyramids in the aforementioned cities and were reached by climbing steep-side staircases.

The Mayans used a system of picture symbols called glyph (picture) and they wrote in stitched books called codexes, using paper made from fig-tree bark. Three of their books have survived. "They are books of ritual and from them something has been learned about their chronology."[2]

The earliest known form of Mayan writing is thought to date about 200 B.C.E.

The earliest known Mayan calendar inscriptions were found at Chiapa de Carzo in 36 B.C.E.

The Mayans were very skilled in mathematics and astronomy, and especially, in the development of a calendar.

Their religion was based on astronomical observation in carrying out ritual and ceremonial acts.

Some scholars think that this was the best evidence of the high standards of their cultures because it was based on the major skill in mathematics which they were noted for.

Even though they were skilled craftsmen who exported elaborate objects carved in jade to other countries in Central America, they were unable to discover the arch or wheel.

Mayan society in this classical era was probably ruled by hereditary priests and noble warriors.

The Mayans were ruled by a Theocracy that was a combination of religious and civic authority over the people. These theocrats prescribed the duties of the priests and scribes who, in turn, administered the governing of the various cities and towns.

The Mayan culture was based on a foundation of religious beliefs. They worshiped serpent gods and jaguar deities. The temples which were erected on top of the pyramids were used to perform human sacrifices to the gods.

The Mayans were very warlike and they found it necessary to supply captives for their human sacrifices to the gods. They offered these sacrifices to the gods according to astronomical calendar dates or to remember royal funerals.

Victims had their hearts cut out and shown to the populace. These bloody ceremonies were controlled by priests.

Bloodletting even encompassed the royal kings. Their tongues were pierced with cords barbed with thorns. This act was used to

---

[2]   Roberts, J.M. A Concise History of the World. New York, Oxford University Press, 1993.

sustain the gods who, in turn, underwent ritual sacrifices in order to sustain the human race.

They Mayans like the Olmecs participated in a ball game. The only difference was that this game was similar to basketball. The object of the game was to knock the solid rubber ball through stone rings which were set high on the court walls. Players couldn't touch the ball with their hands. They could only use their knees and hips. They wore protective clothing which included a heavy belt. This belt was made of leather and wood. They also wore gloves, leather hip-pads, and kneepads.

The game was literally one of death for carvings on the walls at Chichen Itza show the winning team sacrificing a defeated opponent by cutting his head off.

In Mesoamerica, the heart of a losing captain was sometimes cut out which shows their war-like nature.

The Mayans drained swamps to increase their agricultural productivity which consisted mainly of the growth of corn (maize).

There was a huge increase in the population of the cities which resulted in a shortage of resources.

In the years after 800 C.E., war and famine, due to over cultivation of the land, may have been the cause of the collapse of the Mayan cities which led to their desertion.

It might have been caused by a great earthquake or eruption which occurred about the 10th century. Shortly thereafter, invasions by peoples from the Mexican plateau could have caused its collapse. Another possibility may have been disease.

Most likely for its collapse was due to the war-like Toltecs who about 930 C.E. occupied Chichen Itza and later founded their own capital of Tollan or Tula, the 'city of reeds' located approximately 50 miles from present-day Mexico City.

The highland settlements survived a little bit longer but were eventually conquered by the Spanish in the 16th century.

The Mayans will go down in history noted for their art works, architecture (mainly the pyramid temples), a language which is still spoken today by several million people, and especially, for their calendar and mathematics which are used today with some modifications.

ASSYRIAN EMPIRE

Assyrian rule was dominated by militarism whose people used unusual tactics in war which conquered other regions. Other kingdoms feared them because of their reputation of blood thirstiness and brutality. "No city or region they conquered could expect any mercy."

This kingdom has had a long history of conquest since its existence in Mesopotamia about 2000 B.C.E. It was during the tenth century that the kings began to expand their territory in order to control trade routes and to protect their territories.

Over the next 200 years, the Assyrian armies because of their conquests enabled the Empire to reach its zenith. Their kingdom stretched from the borders of Egypt to the Persian Gulf and to Mount Ararat in the north.

It encompassed the great lands of Mesopotamia, Judah, Egypt and Israel.

In 911 B.C.E., King Adadnirari II ascended the throne. It was due to his magnificent rule that brought the Empire its supremacy.

Another great king who added supremacy to the kingdom was the Assyrian warrior king, Tiglath-Pileser III (745-27 B.C.E.). His armies conquered parts of Palestine, Armenia, Syria and annexed Babylonia. He appointed Assyrian rulers to govern the lands they conquered.

The Assyrians were the first to use the chariot in war. These were brilliantly painted wood, metal-covered and carried a driver, an archer and a shield bearer.

These chariots carried the soldiers into battle before they were dismounted to fight. The infantry used metal breastplates and conical helmets for protection. Their siege engines were made of iron which were used to batter down walls of castles.

These chariots revolutionized warfare. They were drawn by four asses. The soldiers were given spears and javelins and a shield for protection.

This array of weaponry struck fear in the enemy and, in some cases, the enemy gave up without a fight.

In the 9th century B.C.E., Babylon was governed by the Assyrians but it remained shaky under its control. After several attempts to throw off the shackles of Assyrian control, King Sennacherib, in 689 B.C.E., destroyed Babylon. The statute of Marduk (the god who created both the earth and human race) was taken to Nineveh, the Assyrian capital. The temples were destroyed and the Assyrians diverted the waters of the Euphrates River to flow over city's site and destroy it.

The city of Babylon was restored by Sennacherib's son, Esarhaddon who by the 7th century B.C.E. had restored the Babylonian kingdom.

It is interesting to note that the famous legendary story of Gilgamesh which is regarded as the oldest epic ever written, gave an account of the Flood and was recorded on 12 cuneiform tablets by the scholars of the last Assyrian king, Ashurbanipal, who died in the year 626 B.C.E. This famous epic tells the story of Gilgamesh the Mighty Warrior who was created by the gods as a perfectly formed man who contained both beauty and courage.

The Assyrians did promote a very efficient central government and improved the roads in its kingdom, achievements worth mentioning.

By 639 B.C.E., the Assyrian king, Ashurbanipal, was able to secure the boundaries of the Empire. He did this with the aid of the Lydians with whom he allied. Also, he established good friendly relations with the war-like Scythians and the Babylonians.

After his death, the Empire began to crumble due to civil war. The Babylonian rebels were supported by the Chaldeans and the Medes in the overthrow of the Empire.

The king of Babylon, Nabopolassar, allied with Cyaxares the Mede, was instrumental in the collapse of the Empire.

In 616 B.C.E., after Nabopolassar defeated the Assyrians at Kablinu, he sacked Ashur, a city in Assyria in the year 614 B.C.E.

It was an alliance with the Scythians in 612 B.C.E. that did the trick and caused the Nineveh capital to capitulate. It was during this time that the last Assyrian king, Sin-Shar-Ishkun killed himself.

Nothing good can be said of this war-like kingdom who believed in warfare to accomplish its objectives.

ROMAN EMPIRE

One of the greatest empires of ancient times was, without question, Rome. It is interesting to note how this civilization came into being. Legends have been told that in the year 753 B.C.E. the twin brothers, Romulus and Remus founded the city of Rome. According to legend the orphaned twins were suckled by a she-wolf who took care of the abandoned boys.

This legend seems a little too far fetch to take very seriously. A more comprehensible account which has been given through historical records and archaeological findings indicate that Latium and Oscan tribes migrated and finally settled in the Italian Peninsula from 2000 to 1000 B.C.E.

About 500 B.C.E. a tribe called the Etruscans invaded the peninsula and conquered the Oscan and Latium tribes. They were given the name of Romans since they colonized the city of Rome. Little is known about this tribe and what we have learned about them comes from the Romans themselves. They captured the city of Rome around 620 B.C.E. and an Etruscan family, called the Tarquins, became kings over Rome. One such king, named Tarquin the Proud, was very cruel and treated the Romans very unkindly. This bitter treatment of the Romans didn't last long for, by 509, they rose up and overthrew this wicked and violent tyrant. They declared Rome a republic and took control of the Italian Peninsula.

The Romans were able to develop a stable and an efficient government. It was organized into two branches—executive and the legislative. At the head of the executive branch was the office of the Consul and the legislative branch consisted of the Senate and the

Assembly of Centuries which was made up of 100 men. The Senate consisted of 300 members who served for life.

The Senate was dominated by the wealthy aristocrats called the patricians. The middle class called the plebeians didn't have much clout in government affairs as the patricians so, they resented their role in government and were in a constant struggle with the patricians over power.

In order to soften the harshness and brevity toward the plebeians in governmental affairs, the patricians went ahead and established the Office of Tribune, whereby, they finally had veto power over any law passed by the Senate.

One great asset can be attributed to the Romans and that was their establishment of an impressive law code. In 451 B.C.E., Twelve Tables were engraved on bronze tablets and were placed throughout the republic so that everyone could see. Later on, this code became the model for legal systems in Europe and in Latin America.

About 300 B.C.E., the Romans came into contact with the Greeks. They not only adopted their mythology, but also, some of their ideas as well.

After controlling the Italian peninsula by 275 B.C.E., the Romans set their eyes on overseas expansion. This brought on the Punic Wars with Carthage. This conflict began over trading interests with the island of Sicily. This engagement lasted for 23 years as to whom would possess the commerce in the Mediterranean Sea.

In the end, Hannibal lost his territory in Spain and was stopped after he was successful in conquering territory in Italy. The famous Roman general, Scipio, had a plan which forced Hannibal to return to Carthage to protect his country from a Roman invasion. At the famous battle of Zama, Scipio defeated Hannibal forcing Carthage to sue for peace.

Still fearing the Carthagians, the Romans in 146 B.C.E. invaded Carthage and this time burnt it to the ground. Not satisfied with this victory, the Romans went ahead and placed salt on the soil to prevent the growth of plant life. Then, they took all the men, women and children and sold them into slavery.

This expansion of the Roman republic brought on a whole host of problems. The people in the conquered provinces resented their captivity and exploitation and armed resistance followed which required a much larger army to quell any uprising. This brought on an increase in taxes to supply the necessary troops which caused resentment among the population.

An increase in slaves created a labor problem which caused the unemployment of many Roman citizens. Many farmers left their land and migrated to the cities which caused a food shortage. This resulted in food production which was in the grasp of wealthy landowners.

The army became inflated with professional soldiers because of the long campaigns they had to fight. This eliminated the small farmers who closed the military ranks during the short terms in which they volunteered their services.

These problems were rectified to some degree when two brothers and two generals came to the fore. The brothers were Tiberius and Gaius Gracchus, the grandsons of the great General Scipio.

These brothers were disliked by the patricians because they were helping the poor so, they organized riots which resulted in the deaths of these two magnificent brothers.

The two generals were Marius and Sulla which tried different strategies to end the economic crisis which hit the republic. These two men did little to solve the problems of the republic.

The two generals were followed by three outstanding military and political leaders who formed the First Triumvirate. They were Crassus, Julius Caesar and Pompey. In 60 B.C.E. they took over the reins of the Roman government.

Julius Caesar had his eyes on a one-man rule of the Roman government, and therefore, had to eliminate his colleagues. Crassus was killed in battle in 53 B.C.E. and this left only Pompey to contend with. He finally cornered and defeated Pompey who was murdered in Egypt.

After Caesar conquered Gaul (France), the Senate, fearing that Caesar might seize power in Rome, sent word to him to stay north of the Rubicon River.

As many historical 'buffs' know Caesar's reply: "The die is cast." He entered Rome in triumph and in 45 B.C.E. took the position of dictator for life which ultimately weakened the Senate's power. The Senate took immediate action and had Caesar stabbed to death on the Senate floor. The end of the republic came when Octavian, grandnephew and adopted son of Caesar, formed the Second

Triumvirate with Mark Antony and Lepidus. These three men divided the Roman Empire into three parts. This arrangement didn't last long as Octavian wanted more power. He finally accomplished this end when in 31 B.C.E. he defeated Mark Antony in Egypt.

Octavian took the name of Augustus Caesar while he was in Rome. He ruled Rome from 27 B.C.E. to 14 C.E. During this period of time, he took away much power from the Senate and became the sole law executor and lawmaker which resulted in the termination of representative government of the republic. During his reign, Rome experienced 200 years of relative peace which has been called the Pax Romana or Roman Peace.

From 14 to 68 C.E. the Roman Empire was ruled by four emperors who were called the Julian emperors because they were all related to Julius Caesar.

These four emperors who were regarded as bad because of their treachery or madness and instability, were followed by "Five Good Emperors." They were Nerva, Trajan, Hadrian, Antonius Pius and Marcus Aurelius who brought stability, order and wealth to the empire.

These emperors made all conquered peoples citizens of Rome. They were granted all the privileges and rights which citizens usually have. By granting these rights, the emperors were smart enough to gain the loyalty of all citizens in the various provinces, who provided safety and security of their vast domains. Also, they were given the privilege of joining the Roman legions which were the best of the times.

During the Pax Romana (Roman Peace), cultural advancement reached its peak. They built the Pantheon in 128 C.E., and also, constructed the Appian Way, one of the first major roadways. From the Greeks, they acquired a great deal of knowledge which they put to use.

In matters of religion, they began to put away their adoration and worship of gods and goddesses and accepted a new religion, Christianity. The Romans tolerated other religions as well. "These religions were required to perform the prescribed rituals at the appropriate times."

By the fourth century C.E. a majority of citizens in the Roman Empire had converted to Christianity. Emperor Constantine, who later became a Christian himself, issued the Edict of Milan in 313 B.C. This Edict granted tolerance for the new religion.

Emperor Theodosius the Great adopted Christianity which became the official religion of the Roman Empire.

As with all good things the end was inevitable. The fall of the Roman Empire is thought to have occurred in the fifth century when Attila the Hun, who came from Asia, forced a Germanic tribe, the Visigoths, into Roman territory. They invaded the Italian Peninsular and sacked Rome.

A Germanic tribe called the Vandals invaded the Roman Empire in 455, and sacked Rome. In 476, a German chieftain, named Odoacer, deposed the last emperor. This date is recorded when the Roman Empire collapsed.

There has been much speculation among historians as to what caused the fall of the Roman Empire. Several factors have been recorded which might have prevailed in this disaster.

"First of all, some think that the Christian religion may have caused its downfall as this led to Romans spending more time thinking about the afterlife rather than concentrating on the problems at hand. Second, others believe it was caused by a series of successive plaques. Third, some think that slavery was an important factor as the Romans became lazy and unemployed. Fourth, some think it might have been a decline in traditional Roman values which were linked with the simple agrarian lifestyle of the Roman republic. Fifth, it might have been caused from lead poisoning from indoor plumbing. Sixth, there was corruption in the government and the army. Seventh, civil wars left the empire poorly defended against enemy forces." Eight, new evidence have shown that the anopheles mosquito may have been the cause which may have weaken the army to the extent that when the German barbarians attacked, they were so weak from malaria, they were unable to fight.

This theory has a lot to be said for this author witnessed marines of the 4th Marine Division during WWII who contracted malaria and were unable to fight on the islands in the Pacific, namely Saipan, Tinian and Iwo Jima.

MACEDONIAN EMPIRE

One of the greatest empires of ancient times can be attributed to that military genius, Alexander the Great. He was the son of another great military commander, Philip II of Macedonia and his wife Olympias, the daughter of Neptolemus of Epirus.

By reorganizing and enlarging his army, he was able to improve it so that it became a great fighting force. He first used this mighty fighting machine to conquer the regions north of Greece and then Greece itself.

As the leader of the Greek city-states, he organized them into a federation. His next move was to wage war on the vast Persian Empire but was cut short because he was assassinated in 336 B.C.E. He was only forty-six years old.

His son, Alexander, succeeded to the throne after his death. He was only twenty years old at the time.

Alexander grew up in Athens and his father made sure that his son would receive an education worthy of a king so he hired as his teacher the great philosopher, Aristotle.

Although Alexander ruled for only thirteen years, he was able to build an empire greater than any that had yet existed.

Alexander took up the reins of the army and proceeded to accomplish what his father had in mind, the conquest of Persia. Before doing this, however, he had to put down a rebellion in mainland Greece. In a ferocious campaign, he stormed the city of Thebes killing 6,000 of its citizens. Because of the unmerciful onslaught, no Greek city afterwards dared to refuse his commands.

With an army about 35,000 he set out to conquer the Persian Empire which at that time included both Asia Minor and Egypt. He was able with this impregnable force to defeat large Persian armies at Halicarnassus, Granicus, and Miletus. After these victories he moved down the coast of the Mediterranean toward Egypt.

On the way, the Phoenician city of Tyre, located on an island, tried to hold out against this belligerent ruler.

Alexander had his men build a causeway from the mainland to Tyre. After it was built, his army proceeded across it and was able to sack the city. After killing a great number of civilians, he took 30,000 inhabitants and sold them as slaves.

From 334-330 B.C.E., he conquered Turkey, Phoenicia, Syria, Persia and Egypt where he founded the city of Alexandria (named after him) noted for its great library.

After a two-month siege, Gaza fell. Egypt surrendered without a fight and he was crowned pharaoh and was declared a god.

From Egypt he led his troops back into Asia and at Arbela, in 331 B.C.E., he defeated a huge Persian army.

After this major victory, he led his troops into Babylon and then into the Persian capitals of Persepolis and Susa. In Persepolis, he burned the palace. Alexander proceeded to Persia and defeated Darius III at the Battle of Issus River in Syria. He defeated Darius again at the Battle of Gaugamela and took control of the Persian Empire. To complete his conquest of the Persian Empire, he led his forces into Afghanistan and Uzbekistan, and also, into Bactria. The Macedonian army, for more than three years, campaigned continuously through central Asia. He fought his last battle near the banks of the Indus River. He decided to invade northern India but his troops refused to go any further as they were exhausted from previous battles and he was forced to agree with their demands to return home.

Disgruntled at his men, he led them through the arid Gedrosian Desert near Iran. In 323 B.C.E. he reached the famous city of Babylon where he died at the age of 32. There has been much speculation for the cause of his death. Some writers say he died of a fever and others say he drank too much.

His empire ended after his death and his generals seized his territory during the Wars of the Diadochi ("Wars of the Successors") after his mad brother and an infant son were murdered. For several centuries after his death, the Greek language, sculpture, architecture, learning and cultural pursuits dominated much of the ancient world. Historians have aptly called this era the Hellenistic Age.

Alexander has been especially noted for fusing his great empire into two parts by creating a joint Graeco-Persian kingdom and culture. At the head of this vast domain, he intended to make himself ruler. This assimilation was accomplished by enlisting great numbers of Persians into his notable army and second, by having several thousand of his Macedonian troops marry Persian women. He set an example for his troops by marrying the daughter of Darius even though he had previously married an Asian princess.

Alexander has gone down in history as a great general who possessed a powerful personality. His troops looked upon him as a god. His bravery knew no bounds. He was constantly up front in battle and his men recognized his bravery and courage which increased their morale and strengthened their courage. He shared the spoils of war with his men and their hardships which showed his generosity and his feelings toward his troops.

AZTEC EMPIRE

The Aztec nomads settled in the Valley of Mexico in the 13 century. They were wanderers who build their homes on two marshy islands in the south of Lake Texcoco. In order to fill the marshy islands and promote futile raised fields called "chinampas", they had to float large baskets of earth. These fields produced maize and other staple crops.

To keep the artificial plots of land in place, they had to plant trees.

The Aztecs used a calendar stone to tell them when to plant and harvest. Calendar stones had a picture for everyday. They divided a 365 day year into 18 months of 20 days each.

In 1325 these nomads founded the city of Tenochtitlan on islands in Lake Texcoco.

According to Aztec legend, to show priest-leaders where to build this city, a war god gave them a sign, an eagle on a cactus.

The site was divided into four quarters within which were separate districts for each family group.

A priest-king called Tenoch was Tenochtitlan first ruler who died about 1370 C.E.

The Aztecs spoke Nahautl which was the language of the Toltecs. They forged alliances with powerful leaders of local warring tribes in order to protect their new settlements. They, themselves, were fierce warriors and, because of their conquests of other tribes, they became a major power in Central America. At times, they became mercenaries for other regions.

The Aztecs were known for their development of a tribute system which they imposed on conquered peoples. The conquered were also forced to perform military service and surrender their lands.

These tactics enabled them to ensure their dominance for a short period of times.

The local rulers were used as tax collectors, thereby, permitting them to maintain their positions. By performing this function, they were given protection by the Aztecs.

The Aztec king, Itzcoatl, in 1426, formed an alliance with the states of Tlacopan and Texcoco and with these forces they were able to overthrow the powerful Tepanecs. This campaign gave them a vast domain. They became wealthy by engaging and operating a vast network of trade caravans which were controlled by a merchants' guild, the pochteca.

They were also great architects and built splendid palaces, temples, and pyramids.

The Aztecs had built a military force by sending boys to military schools where they were trained to fight in very difficult terrain in central Mexico.

These young boys were taught endurance by going on long marches carrying on their persons heavy supplies. To train for actual combat, they were given wooden clubs and spears from which the obsidian blades had been removed.

In actual combat, spies were sent out to discover the enemy's positions. Also, to secure a best place for an attack.

These spies consisted of 'Ocelot' warriors. The best fighters were the "Eagle" warriors who were in the forefront of an attack. These confrontations were bloody. Prisoners were sometimes taken to the temple at Tenochtitlan where human sacrifices were made.

Sometimes as many as 20,000 were sacrificed in one day.

The Aztecs believed that they lived in the world called the "Fifth Sun" and this world would eventually be destroyed.

This sun god, Huitzilopochtli, had to be fed daily in order to be content. Therefore they believed it was their sacred duty to provide this god with chalchiuhuatl, a form of nectar found in human blood.

They thought the whole universe would fail to function without this blood. The human heart was considered life itself and Huitzilopochtli needed to be fed human hearts and blood so that he would not impose his anger on them.

"The warriors business was to feed the sun and their search for victims was looked upon with great honor."

The Aztec religion was very complex and had at least 128 major deities. Each deity's function was to serve as patrons of cities and various jobs.

Various ceremonies and festivals, which involved dancing, feasting, and human sacrifices, were religious observances.

Nezhualcoyotl's writings were skeptical of the existence of the pantheon of Aztec gods. His writings have even hinted to a monotheistic deity which gave meaning to existence.

Throughout Mesoamerica, groups of related myths helped to integrate the natural world of the creator. By putting society at the center of the universe, they were able to do this. They also placed sacredness on the activities of the upper social class and their hierarchy.

In the Mesoamerican viewpoint, the spiritual parameters between death and life were unclear. They believed that their gods, humans, ancestors, and animals could live in a spiritual form and, when necessary, change their external appearances.

The source of their practice of human sacrifice, in which the hearts of victims were cut out with obsidian knives, was based on the creation myth when the god Nanahuatzin hurled himself into a blazing fire and was unbelievably transformed into the rising sun. Because the sun does not move, the other gods had to give their blood so that he received the energy which was needed for his daily trip across the sky.

It has been estimated that as many as 50,000 human sacrifices were performed each year. These sacrifices were necessary for, if their sun god, Huitzilopochtli, didn't receive sufficient hearts, he wouldn't have the energy to awaken again the next day.

The social structures of the Aztecs were very similar to previous civilizations. At the top of the scale were the king and his family. They represented the earthly gods. Next, were the nobility which composed a majority of soldiers whose importance was based on how many prisoners of war were taken for human sacrifice. The most noblest way to die was while taking prisoners for sacrifice. This was called a "flowery death." The nobles were followed by artisans and scribes. A special merchant class called the pochteca traded luxury items.

At the bottom of the heap were the peasants who worked in the fields to produce the necessary agricultural products, mostly maize.

It is interesting to note how superstitious the Aztecs were. They believed in magic, sorcery, witchcraft, and in spirits. Nothing could be done until the astrologer—priest had consulted the stars to see if the time was ripe.

The Aztec healer or <u>ticitl</u> used trickery along with a little knowledge of curing herbs along with incantations and magic spells to cure illness and disease.

The Aztecs regarded sickness as a divine punishment or because of a curse from a wicked spirit.

The decline of the empire came quickly. There were several factors which caused its demise. First, their tribute system of their conquered peoples caused resentment and animosity, but most of all, these people had to offer themselves for human sacrifice which the Aztecs needed to appease their gods, particularly, their sun god, Huitzilopochtli.

Second, they lacked the technology to prepare their food which became laborious and lasting, especially, without the use of the wheel. As the Empire grew in population, this lengthy performance in food production was taxing on the populace and caused an internal weakness and lethargy.

Third, and the most significant reason, was the invasion of the Spanish in the 16th century (1519). Montezuma II, ruler of the Aztecs, had to submit to the Spanish general, Hernan Cortés.

Montezuma, thinking him to be a god who was supposed to come to their land, gracefully received him with open arms. Montezuma was taken prisoner and was later murdered. Cortés was able to take the capital city of Tenochtitlan in 1519 with the aid of the states of Tlaxcala and Mixtec which hated Montezuma. This famous city was destroyed in the process.

Thus, a belligerent and blood-thirsty civilization came to a horrific end.

MONGOLIAN EMPIRE

When one reads about the Mongolian Empire, the great and notorious ruler, Genghis Khan comes to mind. His greatness lies in his vast domain which stretched from Asia, across Russia, into Persia and then into Hungary and Poland in Europe. Because of his conquests, he became known as the Great Khan by a general assembly of chiefs (assembly called a kuriltai) in 1206. He was regarded as notorious and cruel because of a terrible policy he invoked called retribution.

During his campaigns, when he encountered his enemy, he gave them a choice of either surrendering or be killed if they resisted.

Genghis was born on the Onon River in Mongolia in 1167, the son of a great chief who had ruled an extensive piece of land from the Amur River to the Great Wall of China.

Genghis's real name was Temujin and he succeeded his father at the age of 13. With his military victory in 1203 against the Keraites, his people then honored him with the title Genghis Khan ("mighty ruler").

His first campaign was in 1207 when his armies struck the Tangut kingdom of Xi Xia in northwest China.

After tasting a victory in China, he gobbled up the powerful Qin Empire formed by the Manchu-related Jurchens.

It was during these ghastly campaigns that entire towns were demolished and its civilians, men, women, and children were slaughtered. This was the time when his policy of retribution went into effect. This policy preceded his advancement and many towns and cities, because of fear, automatically surrendered without a fight.

The Kara Khitai Empire was one of these people who were subdued because of his horrific policy of destruction in 1219.

Not satisfied with this operation of destruction, he then, in 1227, destroyed the Khwarazm Empire which resulted in his empire stretching from eastern Persia to the North China Sea.

The policy of retribution was not the only tactic he used in conquering his enemy. He was a military genius when it came to military tactics. For instance, during battle he would retreat giving the impression of defeat. When the enemy pursued the retreating Mongolian army, his other army units would out-flank and surround the confused enemy.

His army, which was at one time nomadic livestock herders on the Central Asian grasslands, turned out to be well-organized, fearful warriors. Because they did a lot of hunting for food, they became very adept with the bow and arrow which they used while riding on their small stallions during battle.

Temujin was a military genius as he turned these shepherds into a well-organized army by uniting these various feuding clans.

After his capture of the Islamic Khwarazm Shah's empire, he led a raid into Afghanistan and northern India.

By 1227, the Mongolian Empire stretched from eastern Persia to the North China Sea.

After he had established his Mongolian Empire, he created a capital at the city of Karakorum. Here, he developed sound policies of government which were very progressive. He was smart enough to consult Chinese Confucian scholars and Muslim engineers to build his capital city. Also, he invoked a policy of religious tolerance throughout his empire which was a beneficial factor in ruling so many diverse cultures. Because he brought peace to Asia, it has been regarded or referred to as <u>Pax Mongolia</u> or Mongolian peace.

The people of his empire were protected by his army and this sense of security enabled his empire to prosper in trade and commerce. This revitalization of commerce had its effect on the Silk Road which was used considerably in the transactions of trade throughout the Middle East, Asia, Africa, and Europe.

In 1226, he conquered China which he wanted to do much earlier. With a huge army he was successful in this campaign but, he wasn't to enjoy the fruits of his labor as he died in 1227 as China was on the verge of collapse. His body was escorted to the capital city of Karakorum for burial.

However, his third son, Ogedei was able to consolidate Genghis Empire and was happy to stay home rather than pursue other conquests.

However, his sons, Batu, Hulegu, and Kublai were not satisfied with their father's state of affairs, and therefore, they pursued their conquests in the Middle East, Asia, and parts of Europe which expanded the Mongolian Empire.

It was Kublai, however, who established the Yuan dynasty and established the capital at Tatu which is present day Beijing.

However, Kublai ran into trouble with the Chinese because the Mongols resisted the Chinese culture and placed a distance between them and the Chinese in their ideas and placement of officials in the realm.

Also, the Mongolians helped the merchant and artisan classes who, "according to Confucian Chinese standards, were at the bottom of the Chinese social structure." Because of these conditions, Kublai had alienated the gentry class of Chinese society which held a very high position in China.

It was at this juncture that the Chinese took action and overthrew the Yuan dynasty and began the famous Ming dynasty.

After this takeover, the Mongolians returned to Mongolia and, as a result, their power in Asia came to an end.

Nevertheless, Genghis can be remembered for his tolerance of other people's religions and his acceptance of their ideas. These conquered people were thus able to centralize their government over diverse people and vast territories.

OTTOMAN EMPIRE

The Ottomans were Turkic people who came from the Anatolian Peninsula in the northwest during the thirteen century. Osman, an Ottoman leader, was the founder of the Turkish dynasty.

The early Ottomans were ghazis (warriors) whose job was fighting for Islam and winning converts. They made constant attacks in Asia Minor and the Balkans during the 14th century.

In 1354 they captured the Gallipoli Peninsula on the European side of the Dardanelles which gave them a permanent base in Europe.

Osman created an empire in the fourteenth century when he added additional territory in the capture of the declining Seljuk Empire. Originally, the Ottomans had served the Seljuks who had established themselves in Central Asia and the Middle East and gave the caliphate an extraordinary administrative structure.

In 1055, the Seljuks became the official protectors of the caliphate and controlled the Islamic East.

In 1097, the Crusaders pledged an oath of allegiance to the Byzantine emperor by which they did battle against the Seljuks and were able to take Jerusalem in 1099 under the leadership of Godfrey of Bouillon. In the 12th century, the Crusaders fought against the Ayyubids, who had ousted the Seljuks as the supreme power in the Middle East.

In 1361, Murad I, the greatest of the early Ottoman sultans, captured Adrianople in present-day Bulgaria. This city was ranked second as the most important in the Byzantine Empire. Murad renamed this city Edirne and made it his capital.

In 1389, at the Battle of Kosovo in Serbia, he was killed but gained a great victory. He was followed in the empire by his grandson, Murad II who expanded the empire. A corps of soldiers called the janissaries gave him much support during his rule. They consisted of Christian slaves and converts to Islam. Their function was to serve the sultan as his personal guard. They were forbidden to marry and were cut off from civil society.

In order to acquire a steady flow of recruits, Murad II devised a system called <u>devshirme</u> in which Christian youths were sent from the Balkans to the sultan's capital each year.

After receiving military training, their duty was to serve the sultan for the rest of their life. Before this extensive training, they had to be converted to the Islamic religion.

The janissaries, although they were slaves, could gain high positions in government, including wealth in the empire.

Murad II's thirst for conquest was insatiable so, he launched campaigns in Albania, Serbia, Walachia (now southern Romania) and Greece. His next stop was the famous city of Constantinople, which had weakened to such a degree, was on the verge of decline and was ripe for conquest. This fall took place in 1453 when a 20 year old sultan, Mehmed II, stormed the walls of Constantinople and, after a 53 day siege, brought an end to a magnificent city.

After its downfall, the city became known as Istanbul and became the residence of the Ottoman sultans and their capital.

The Ottomans were still hungry for more land. So, from 1514 to 1517, the Sultan Selim I launched attacks into Egypt, Arabia, and Mesopotamia. They were able to control Mecca, Medina, and Jerusalem.

After his capture of North Africa, he was heralded as the new defender of Islam and was declared its caliph.

After the expansion of the empire into North Africa and the Middle East, Suleiman I was called by several different names. One was "al-Qanuni," the Law-giver. Another "The Magnificent" by the Europeans.

His armies, in 1526, defeated Hungary in the Battle of Mohacs. Three years later in 1529, he besieged Vienna. It was here that his armies were finally defeated due to the combined effort of several German princes and the Holy Roman Emperor.

Not successful here, the Turkish navy tried their luck of expansion in the Mediterranean Sea in 1571.

However, a brave and courageous man, named Don John of Austria, led a Christian navy at the Battle of Lepanto which stopped their encroachment in these waters.

Thus, by the late 17th century, the Turks had been pushed out of Hungary.

By 1600, the Ottoman Empire began to decline.

The final collapse of the Ottoman occurred with the allied victory in WWI.

It was during this time that a courageous and determined soldier named Kemal Ataturk who fought in the war against allied forces consisting of British and New Zealand and Australians (known as Anzacs), defeated them in the battle of Gallipoli in 1915. It was he who fought for the independence of Turkey after the war. After ousting the Greeks from Turkish territory in 1923, as president, he proclaimed the Republic of Turkey.

In the final analysis, there were many achievements of the Ottoman Empire. This was due mainly because of its administrative structure. At its head was the sultan, a hereditary ruler, who had supreme authority in military and political affairs. A grand vizier, whose function was to advise the sultans with the backing of an imperial council in matters which related to state diplomacy. Their duties were to control the bureaucracy which was divided into districts and provinces.

These districts and provinces were governed by pashas. Their duties were to collect taxes, maintain law and order, and supply armies when needed. For doing these administrative duties, they were given land by the sultan.

These pashas were supported by a queen who was the mother of the sultan. She administered, mainly, as an advisor to the throne.

Women, incidentally, were treated more leniently than in other religions and were given more freedoms. For instance, they were allowed to own and inherit property. Also, they could not be forced into marriage

The social structure might be regarded as standard for this era.

At the peak of the mass was the ruling class followed by the merchants who were exempted from paying government taxes. They, in turn, were followed by artisans, peasants and nomads who were at the bottom of the ladder.

As for religion, the Sunni Muslims were the majority in the Ottoman Empire.

VIKING EMPIRE

The Vikings began raiding Western Europe from their homeland, Scandinavia during the eighth century. These people were the Norsemen—Norwegians, Danes and Swedes who raided and traded in northern Europe from 800-1100 C.E. These warrior people were like pirates who traveled down the European coastline and sailed up river deep into the heartland of Europe where they plundered and pillaged.

They pillaged mostly the monasteries because of their lack of protection and their housing of gold and silver vessels. These monasteries were located on some islands—Jarrow, Lindisfarne, and Iona. They also conquered northern France and these Norsemen, or Normans, later built a fleet of ships which brought William the Conqueror to England in 1066 C.E.

The boats that they used to sail up the rivers of Europe were known as dragon boats.

Some of these Vikings did settle on the lands they conquered and became upright citizens. Others took delight in fighting and plundering.

In 789 C.E., they were seen off the Dorset Coast. In the following decade, they went on a rampage and attacked the Irish, English, and French coasts. Then, they sacked Utrecht, invaded Ireland, and plundered Canterbury and London.

Normandy, in 911 C.E., was relinquished to them.

The English and the Franks by the end of the ninth century had learned to get along with this warlike people.

In England, Alfred the Great, in order to protect his kingdom, built a huge force of soldiers and a large fleet to counter any Viking attacks.

In France, along the Loire and Seine Rivers, Charles the Bald also took precautions to defend his domain by building a series of fortifications.

Canute the Great had joined the "band wagon" to protect his kingdom in the North Sea which included Norway and Denmark.

He did this by arranging alliances with the Scandinavian civilizations and the Normans.

Unfortunately, his empire collapsed after his death in 1035 C.E.

The Vikings began to settle down about 850 C.E. and began to engage in trade relations. They had established trade with the Roman Empire by exporting amber.

After the western half of the Roman Empire collapsed in 476 C.E., the Swedish traders looked to the east and established trade with the Byzantine Empire at Constantinople which they found to be very lucrative.

During the 9th century, the Scandinavian kingdoms were engaged in the trading operations at the center of Kiev, Novgorod, and other Russian towns.

The Vikings didn't stop here for, their desire to gain wealth took them across the Atlantic where they established settlements in Iceland. From this staging point, a voyager, Eric the Red, in 982 C.E., reached Greenland where he established a settlement in 986 C.E.

His son, Leif Ericson, in 992 C.E., found land further west called Vinland which may have been the island of Newfoundland or the Labrador region.

He failed to establish a settlement here on account of the hostility of natives whom the Vikings labeled 'skrfllings.'

By the 10th century, a centralized monarchy was established at home. This foundation in government was due mainly through the efforts of the Church and Christianization. These kingdoms in the Empire began a period of expansion, but ran into trouble when they encountered the Hanseatic League which brought their power and authority to a standstill.

The commercial cities of Danzig, Hamburg, and Lubeck formed this League.

One of their functions was to defend their ships called Cogs against attacks by pirates. Another function was the maintainment of strategic ports in Europe.

This League finally declined because of the expansion of the principal trading routes in the Atlantic whose competition was too great to overcome.

Another incident worth mentioning was the Norseman (Vikings) who attacked Paris in 885 C.E. with a force of 40,000 men and 700 vessels. The Parisians were able to endure this onslaught for 10 months.

Because of a lack of food, starvation took hold and the Parisians were forced to eat dogs, rats, cats, acorns, and roots.

This happening shows the barbarism, cruelty and insensitivity of these Vikings.

The Vikings, nevertheless, were hard producing individuals who worked the land to produce barley and oats which they used to make porridge and bread. They bred sheep, goats, cattle, poultry, and pigs. Their habitat consisted of long, rectangular farmhouses, or longhouses. They also made iron tools which were made in the farm's forge.

These hardy people slept on wooden beds or earth benches.

They were not illiterate as someone would thing. They had an alphabet whose letters were called runes. Their messages were carved in runes on metal, stone, and wood. Some of these rune stones reveal stories of their history. They loved to tell stories and poets or skalds told the adventures of Viking heroes and battles. They also told legends about their gods, such as Odin, god of death and battle, and Thor, ruler of the sky.

The climax of the Viking Empire can be said to have occurred about the 9th century when Alfred the Great who became the king of Wessex in 871 C.E., routed the Viking army at the Battle of Ethandune in 878 C.E. By 886 C.E., he captured London and became king of all England. Guthrum, the Viking leader, was permitted to keep the Danelaw which was the northern half of England on condition that he recognizes Alfred as his overlord.

Not much can be said of Viking achievements. They did have accomplished merchants who established trade relations with other countries and they did develop an alphabet with letters called runes which were carved on metal, stones, and wood. They were also noted for their sailing vessels. However, when we speak of the Vikings, we immediately call to mind their brutality, cruelty, and plundering which has left a black mark on their history.

FRANKISH EMPIRE

When the Western Roman Empire collapsed in 476 C.E., the barbarian warlords fought each other incessantly for land and power in the various territories that they once dominated.

The Franks, a Germanic tribe, migrated from central Europe in the early 400's and settled in France.

The most successful king of the Franks was Clovis who ruled from 481 to 511 C.E. His realm extended from modern Belgium to the Mediterranean Sea.

He was one of the early Frankish kings who belonged to the Merovingian Dynasty named for an ancestor call Meroweg.

Gregory of Tours, who wrote the first history of the Merovingian kings, said that they were known as "the long-haired kings" because their hair engraced their shoulders.

Clovis, in 496 C.E. had himself baptized as a Catholic by Bishop Remigius of Reims according to the Catholic tradition.

This move has been taken as a political gesture rather than a religious one because at that time a ruler had to be linked with the church in order to rule most effectively since bishops played an important part in local administration.

He also converted the Frankish kingdom to Christianity. The story has it that on his way to a battle he believed he received God's assistance by a sign he saw in the sky which told him to convert these people.

Clovis was different from other German kings as he encouraged the integration of the Germanic ruling class with the local population in the regions which he conquered.

Clovis was a great leader as well as a great ruler. In the year 486 C.E. he had defeated Syragius, the last Roman general in Gaul, at Soissons in northern France.

After conquering much of central and eastern France, he made his capital at Paris.

With the death of Clovis in 511 C.E., his kingdom was divided between his four sons and the Merovingian monarchy fell into decline. Frankish lands were separated into distinct kingdoms and were constantly at war with one another.

Real authority passed from these <u>rois fainéants</u> ("do-nothing kings") to stewards (mayors of the palace) who were from the royal house.

By the mid-7th century, the mayors of the palace came mostly from the Carolingian family. One of the most outstanding Carolingian mayors was Charles Martel ("the Hammer"). He got this nickname after he defeated an Arab army near Tours in 732 C.E. This was a very important victory as it stopped Islamic forces into Christian Europe.

Charles was a staunch supporter of the church and he was actively engaged in supporting the St. Boniface mission in his conversion of the Germans to Christianity.

He was succeeded by his son Pepin the Short. Pepin obtained permission from the pope in 751 C.E. to depose Childeric III, the Merovingian king. He, then, wanting to be elected king, got an assembly of Franish nobles together to vote for him to be the first ruler of the Carolingian kings. This inaugurated the Carolingian dynasty. He was crowned by the pope in a ceremony at Reims in northern France.

In 768 C.E., Pepin the short died.

Charlemagne or Charles the Great became king of the Frankish empire in 768 C.E., after the death of his brother Carloman. Charles became one of the greatest rulers of medieval Europe.

Charles didn't waste any time in gaining new conquests. He went on and conquered much of western Europe—Lombardy, Bavaria, Saxony, and northeastern Spain.

At the request of Pope Hadrian I, Charles crossed the Alps in 773 C.E. and completely annihilated the kingdom of the Lombards which he fused with his own.

Lombardy and Francia (the land of the Franks) now engulfed the powerful Duchy of Bavaria, a vassal of Charles.

Tassilo, the duke of Bavaria, had to pay homage. Later, he was deposed and exiled to a monastery after a shaky treason trial.

In 778 C.E. Charles was defeated at Roncesvalles after he invaded Spain.

Even though Moorish Spain was unconquered, he was able to establish a frontier zone north of the Ebro River and south of the Pyrenees Mountains.

He, later, waged a full-scale war against the pagan Saxons. He devastated their lands and killed thousands who refused to accept Christianity. Eventually, after this slaughter, they accepted baptism.

Charlemagne, despite of all these handicaps, was able to unite all of these areas under one empire.

In the year 800 C.E. as he knelt at the foot of the alter, Pope Leo III crowned him Emperor of the West.

At this time, he ruled an empire which comprised nearly all Christian Europe.

Frankish law and the courts of justice were established which was a big achievement. A most notable achievement had to do with education. Seeing that he couldn't read, he became very interested in developing schools of education.

He acquired the services of a prominent scholar, Alcuin who ran his Palace School in Aachen and became the minister of education. Alcuin came from Northumbria in England's east coast. He established many schools and established standards in teaching. He had thousands of books from the ancient world copied at his scriptoria. Because of these copyists, Latin classics have been handed down to us.

It was during Charlemagne's grandson, Charles the Bald, that the Carolingian renaissance came into full light.

Charlemagne died in 814 C.E. and was followed by his 36-year-old son, Louis 'The Pious', as emperor. Fortunately, before his death, he was able to crown Louis. Louis's three sons, Lothar, Pepin, and Louis rebelled against him as they felt he was incompetent to rule.

After some fighting, Louis's sons finally signed the Treaty of Verdun in 843 C.E. by which the Frankish Empire was divided into three parts. First part consisted most of present-day France. The second, a large part of Germany. The third, included both northern Italy and a wide segment resting on the French-German border.

At this time, these territories were being invaded by savage intruders. The Vikings from Scandinavia came from the north and the Magyars came from the east.

Some of these Vikings settled in what is now Normandy. The Magyars were defeated by the Saxon king of East Francia, Otto I, at the great Battle of Lechfeld in 955 C.E. Otto I, known as 'Otto the Great' was crowned Roman Emperor in Rome in 962 C.E. From this time on, Germany was to become the center of the empire.

The last group of 9th century invaders were Islamic who from time to time raided the southern coastline of Europe.

Because of these constant raids, travel was at low ebb as people were afraid of traveling and, because of this fear, trade reached a standstill.

The kings' authority became very insignificant as they were unable to protect their people and their property.

Last, but not least, was the development of the system of feudalism which took hold for several centuries and was accompanied by the manorial system which involved the lord of the manor and the peasants.

Much can be said of Charlemagne's character and conquests. He was a devoted Christian and benevolent king who believed it was a sacred duty of a ruler to safeguard the material and spiritual welfare of his people. He was a staunch military leader who expanded his empire by conquests. He traveled widely with his government officials and placed his mark of government throughout his empire.

No wonder he was called Charlemagne the Great.

ARABIAN EMPIRE

The founder of the Islamic religion was Muhammed who was born around 570 C.E. near Mecca in what is now Saudi Arabia.

His parents died when he was a child and he was an orphan at the age of six and grew up under the guidance of other family members who trained him as a merchant. As he grew older he began to travel with his uncle, a trader, throughout the Middle East. It was during these travels that he became acquainted with the Judeo-Christian idea of monotheism.

At the time, the Arabs of Mecca were idol-worshippers and were in constant trouble having quarrels, violence, and disputes.

Muhammed believed that if these people came to believe in one God, like the Christians and Jews, they might be able to solve their problems.

In 610 C.E., while Muhammed was meditating on this problem in a cave on Mount Hira, he had a vision. He said that the Archangel Gabriel had appeared and told him that he had been chosen as the prophet of Allah, the one God. He, with Fatima Ali and his grandchildren al-Hassan and al-Husayn, considered himself the last in the series of prophets—Abraham, Moses, and Jesus.

Muhammed's first converts were Khadijah, his wife, a wealthy widow who made him rich, also, his cousin, Ali, who was converted to the new faith. This idea of monotheism didn't sit well with the Meccans who were polytheists who used the Kaaba for idol worship. Mecca, at this time, was a place of religious pilgrimage for the Bedouins (nomadic people who migrated to different areas in order to feed their sheep). As stated, these people believed in polytheism and animism ("the conviction that life is produced by a spiritual force that is separate from matter").

No wonder a conflict was in the making. Muhammed's message was simple, "there is only one God, Allah, and everyone is equal in his eyes, so everyone should be treated equally."

This message, however, wasn't well taken by the merchants of Mecca who regarded economic inequalities as a means of nature. Muhammed's religion came to be a major threat to the economy of the city because the pilgrims who visited there to worship the shrine of Kaaba were a means of financial assistance for the administration of government.

Because of this financial threat to their revenues, the merchants of Mecca began an era of persecution of the followers of Muhammed, who were called the Muslims.

Because of all this turmoil, Muhammed and his followers left Mecca in the year of 622 C.E. and went to Yathrib, now known as Medina ("city of the Prophet") in his honor. This flight from Mecca is known in history as the hijrah which marks the start of the Muslim calendar—all dates are calculated from this year.

Then, in 624 C.E., the Muslims went to war against the Meccans and defeated them in the Battle of Badr. When they did battle again in 625 C. E., they were utterly defeated at Uhud.

In 627 C.E., in the Battle of the Ditch, again the Meccan army is forced to retreat from Medina. After this victory, Muhammed attacked the chief Jewish tribe because he felt that they were conspiring with the Meccans to do battle with his forces in the Ditch. He, then, became ruthless as he massacred the men involved in the battle and he enslaved both the Jewish women and children.

As a result of this major defeat, the Meccans surrendered their city and the Kaaba to the Muslims.

After this battle, the Meccans accepted him as the city's rightful ruler and he went ahead and consolidated the entire Arabian Peninsula under Islamic rule.

The Islamic religion is based on the Quran (also spelled Koran). The text was written in Arabic and, in order to understand its truth, should only be read in Arabic.

The revelation revealed to Muhammed is contained in this holy book and is regarded as the final authority in matters of faith for the Islamic people. Their lifestyle is also based on this book.

The Quran contains the Five Pillars which are the main guides that Islamic people must follow. Here is a brief synopsis of these pillars.

1. Profession of faith. "There is no God . . ."
2. Pray five times a day
3. Alms giving or <u>zakat</u>—to the poor
4. Required fasting during holy month of Ramadan
5. Pilgrimage if possible, to Mecca or hajj during one's lifetime.

Even though Muslims accept Christians and Jews because they worship the same God, they are referred to, at times, as "People of the Book." However, Muhammed is regarded as the last prophet and Islam is, therefore, the one perfect religion because of him. Muhammed was called the "Seal of the Prophets."

In 632 C.E., Muhammed died and leadership of Islam was handed down to men called caliphs (successor) who were elected for life. Abu Bakr, Muhammed's best friend, was the first of these caliphs. He, in turn, was followed by Umar and Uthman, close friends of Muhammed who became converts of his religion. These caliphs were called "The Rightly Guided Caliphs" because of their religious devotion and their ability to lead.

Because of their wise and intelligent rule, the Islamic state extended to the rest of the Middle East which included North Africa, Persia, Levant (part of Palestine) and Egypt.

After the death of Uthman in 656 C.E., a civil war emerged because of a dispute among Muhammed's family as to whom would succeed him. This dispute also included Muhammed's wife and his son-in-law.

This debate finally came to an end after several years when a man, named Muawiyah, not related to Muhammed's family, proclaimed his entitlement as caliph to the throne. This rule marked the beginning of the Umayyad dynasty and a majority of the Muslims embraced his rule. These Muslims were referred to as the Sunni, or the "People of Tradition and Community."

Because Muawiyah was not related to Muhammed, a group of Muslims did not accept his rule. These groups were the Shiites from Shi' at Ali, or "Party of Ali." They believed that Ali was Muhammed's true successor.

The Umayyad dynasty managed to spread the Islamic faith by conquering other states. However, its regime didn't last long. Under Muawiyah the capital of Islam was moved from Mecca to Damascus in present day Syria. From here, the Umayyad dynasty was able to extend its territory by including all of North Africa and the Middle East.

By conquering Spain, the Islamic faith filtered into the continent of Europe. However, when the Islamic forces tried to conquer France, they were stopped by Charles Martel, a Merovingian ruler, at the Battle of Tours in 732 C.E. After this failure, they proceeded to attack Byzantine Empire. Again they were foiled in this attempt to take this Empire due to the thick walls which surrounded the famous city of Constantinople.

The Umayyad dynasty was due to collapse because of its political philosophy. The government, instead of being based on religion, was politically based and this meant trouble. In matters of religion, the dynasty again came into serious trouble as their philosophy was to accept other religions and to be tolerant thereof; whereas, Muhammed's intent was to convert people to the Islamic faith which was diametrically opposed to this type of philosophy imposed by the Umayyad dynasty. The intent of this type of philosophy was to make it easier to govern conquered territories which seem very plausible considering the times of upheaval. Unfortunately, these converts were taxed to promote and maintain the Islamic aristocracies which were use to luxury and high standards of living.

Because of the imbalance in society and the inequalities of living standards, a change was inevitable.

This change came about in 747 C.E. when the Muslims became disgruntled with the Umayyad rule. This brought about the rise of the Abbasid Dynasty which began to settle in eastern Iran. This family, whose ancestors had been a cousin of Muhammed, joined this group of Muslims and overthrew the Umayyad dynasty in 750 C.E. The capital of the Islamic state was moved to Baghdad which was once a major cultural center of the Old Persian Empire. This dynasty was to last until 1258 C.E. It was during the rule of Harun al-Rashid that Islamic culture reached its zenith and was called its Golden Age. Because it incorporated so many cultures and religions within its borders, it truly became a magnificent civilization that extended globally.

Despite the influence of the dynasties of the Umayyad and Abbasid, the Islamic culture continued to retain its male-dominated customs where equality was ignored when it came to women's rights which were adequately stated in the Quran.

Women were regarded as property and were not to be seen or heard. They received little or no education whereas men, as children, entered school at the age of seven. They were able to continue their studies, if they wished, by entering theological schools where they learned to become leaders in the religious or political arenas of Islamic society.

Despite these inequalities, art, literature and philosophy reached great heights. Calligraphy developed because of the need for religious decoration where human images were banned (Islamic people were iconoclasts). Therefore, the art of arabesque was developed in which this type of art with its intricate geometric designs took hold to create magnificent religious decorations.

The Abbasid period can be glorified because Islamic culture reached its peak when libraries were constructed across the empire. The result of this construction was the advancement in the areas of literature and philosophy.

One of the great achievements of the Arab world was the Shalia mosque with its elaborate dome and minaret which are a typical example of Islamic architecture. It was during Harun's reign that Baghdad became the artistic center of the Muslim world.

After all is said about the Islamic Empire and culture, the leader of this magnificent empire, Muhammed, has gone done in history as a charismatic and charitable ruler whose goal was the conversion of peoples to the Islamic faith and the elevation of the poor to a higher standard of living. He will be truly remembered for his belief in one God, Allah, and his revelations which were written in the Quran, the Islamic Bible.

JAPANESE EMPIRE

The history of Japan is very intriguing and fascinating as it deals with four main islands which were inhabited for at least 50,000 years.

According to archeological evidence, a wave of settlers inhabited Japan during the Paleolithic Age (50,000-1200 B.C.E.).

During the Jomon culture (11,000-300 B.C.E.) more people arrived. The main culture and racial ancestors of the present-day population has been attributed to the Yayoi (300 B.C.E.-300 C.E.).

The Ainu people, who are centered mainly on the island of Hokkaido in the north of Japan and have spread out into the island of Honshu and throughout Japan, are said to have arrived here between 20,000-25,000 B.C.E.

The later Yayoi people migrated to Shokoku, Kyushu, and the peninsula of Kii located near Osaka.

About 300 B.C.E., settlers from mainland Asia migrated to the island of Kyushu in western Japan. The Yayoi people copied the methods of Chinese rice farming, metalworking, and irrigation. These people also made known of the potter's wheel (the making of pottery goes back to 3,000 B.C.E. during the Jomon period in Japan), and their pottery consisted of Japanese people, houses, and animals. They also introduced iron and bronze to Japan in which metal tools, vessels, and weapons were constructed. They buried their dead in funerary urns, wooden coffins, and stone tombs.

In the third century, the Yayoi culture in Japan was engulfed with several changes. The Iron Age developed which increased the production of agriculture. The horse was domesticated which enabled warriors to fight on horseback. More effective armor and weapons were produced which increased the power of the nobles.

The spotlight of this eventual change in their culture occurred mainly in western central Japan. Here, emperors were buried in elaborate burial chambers constructed with large stone blocks and covered with huge earth mounds, or tumuli, reaching 120 feet.

The dead person was accompanied by spears, mirrors, and arms. At his feet, pearl necklaces and funerary pottery were placed with his helmet near his head.

To protect the dead person from evil spirits, clay tomb models, called haniwa, were planted in the earth around the tumulus. Tumuli for burying the dead were at first barrow-shaped, and later, they became square or round. Finally, they took the shape of a keyhole.

In the first century C.E., early settlers from East Asia migrated to Japan. These various clans organized a simple social structure with the aristocrats at the top of the scale followed by artisans, farmers, and servants at the bottom.

It was the ruler of the Yamato clan from the island of Honshu who-united all the clans to become the sole ruler of Japan around 400 C.E.

The Yamato clan, in 604 C.E. began to created imperial power. Yamato Prince Shotokou introduced his Seventeen Article Constitution, or plan of government which declared the power of the emperor to be more dynamic than that of the aristocrats.

During the Taika reforms, the imperial government took over all the land.

Also, Shotoku made the emperor divine.

He also made changes in his administration. He divided the island into administrative districts which were required to pay taxes to the central government. In order to make sure that the people wouldn't go hungry, he took over the farmland.

This act of kindness showed his concern for the welfare of his people.

In 622 C.E., Shotoku died. It was at this time that the Yamato family power declined.

The Fujiwara family seized power in the emperor's court and served as a figurehead of the emperor in order to maintain his sturdy centralized government.

By the end of the 6th century, the Yamato kings had extended their rule over southern Japan and, for a time, over southern Korea.

It was about this time that Buddhism raised its head and had spread to Japan from Korea and China.

About 538 C.E. the monks of China convinced the Japanese court to adopt Buddhism as the official religion of the country. Buddhist temples were constructed and the old temples were knocked down.

Emperor Kotoku, in about 640 C.E., published the Taika Reforms which reorganized the government along Chinese principles. Changes took place—slavery was abolished, universities were established and a civil service took form. Japanese culture in 800 C.E. was entirely influenced by the Chinese.

Chinese script and the Chinese calendar were adopted.

In 710 a permanent imperial court was founded at Heijo (modern Nara). Its foundation took the shape in a pattern of grids similar to that found in the cities of China. Several Buddhist monasteries were built near the city.

Because of the amount of influence that the monks had on the populace, they began to undermine imperial authority. This immediately invoked the services of Emperor Kammu who moved the capital to Heian in 794 to diminish their interference (Heian is present-day Kyoto in Japan).

This action brought a decentralization of government which grew periodically. Because of the weakness of the central government in its administration of the island districts, law and justice fell into the grasp of aristocratic hands. The protection of lands and the people were placed in the hands of hired warriors called <u>samurai</u> ("those who serve"). The samurai developed a code of conduct called <u>bushido</u> (way of the warrior). This code served as a guide for its behavior in Japanese society. Because of the protection the samurai and aristocrats served in Japan's society, a <u>feudal society</u>, similar to those found in medieval Europe, was born.

Unfortunately, this form of society took hold and remained in Japan for the next 400 years.

It was at the end of the twelfth century that a noble named Minamoto Yoritomo centralized the Japanese government in the city of Kamakura. The emperor, whom the Japanese revered, was merely a figurehead and really didn't invoke much authority. The real power was given to a shogun who was a powerful military-leader.

His government called the Kamakura Shogunate controlled Japan from 1192 until 1333.

In the 14ᵗʰ and 15ᵗʰ centuries, the samurais and the aristocrats gained power as the Kamakura Shogunate fell into disrepute.

The aristocrats, called <u>daimyo</u> owned large areas of farmland and had the services of the samurai for protection. These aristocrats got greedy as they tried to capture each other's land which led to a civil war called the Onin War that lasted from 1467 to 1477. The result of all this bloodshed was the collapse of the central government of Japan. The entire islands of Japan became engulfed in a constant state of warfare.

Despite all these hardships, Japan, even to this day, can revel in their artistic accomplishments. They are noted for their paintings, ceramics, gardens with their beautiful flowers, architecture with the pagodas and temples, and most of all, their devotion and respect for their religions—Shinto and Zen Buddhism in which balance and harmony with nature are the focus of art and life.

HUNS EMPIRE

The Huns were a warlike tribe whose origin was Mongolian. By the end of the fourth century, they invaded Europe coming from their Asian lands.

It was their great leader, Attila, who led them in their campaigns against Italy and Gaul (modern day France). After these battles, they settled on the shores of the Danube River.

Attila, known as the "Scourge of God" was a barbarian who pillaged, sacked, and burned the town he conquered.

In the fifth century, he and his brother, Bleda, inherited the kingship of Ruga or Rua. The various Hun tribes were united under Rua's domain and it was he who led his forces against the Eastern Roman Empire. He, also, led his army against the Goths and other peoples in the Balkans.

His victory over the Eastern Roman Empire resulted in the payment of tribute by the emperor Theodosius II in the amount of 350 pounds of gold each year.

After having his brother killed, Attila became the sole ruler and he commenced another attack on Constantinople. This time he exacted an increase tribute of 2,100 pounds of gold a year from Theodosius.

Because of his victories, Attila has been considered by most historians as an astute tactician and a superb mentor when analyzing cavalry performances and logistics.

Over the next ten years, the Huns captured the nations of Italy, Greece, Hungary, and Spain.

From all indications, it seems that the Huns took delight in waging warfare on other countries.

His success can be attributed to his military organization which was based on a tribal system. Each tribe was comprised of about 50,000 soldiers which made up an army called a "tumen" of ten thousand soldiers, A "khan" led each tumen and was the commander of ten thousand horsemen.

These horsemen were well fitted with bows and multiple arrows. The horses, though small in stature, were sturdy and had shaggy hair and wide hooves.

These horses could tolerate extreme temperatures.

After Bleda's death in 445 C.E., the Huns marched on Rome, pillaging and destroying everything on their way.

When they arrived at Troyes in Gaul (France) in 451 C.E., they had plundered Metz and cities in Belgium.

In May of 442 C.E., Attila march on to Orleans to capture the city. Sangiban was the king of the Alans whose monarchy was at Orleans after he was defeated by Aetius, a Roman Commander.

As Aetius marched toward Orleans, he was joined by Theodoric the Visigoth king and Sangiban of the Alans.

The Huns had breached the walls at Orleans when Aetius' army arrived.

After a brief engagement, Attila withdrew his forces northward leaving the Gepid forces at the Seine River to protect his withdrawal.

In a night attack, Aetius destroyed the Gepid forces numbering around 15,000 killed or wounded.

It was at the town of Chalons on the Marne River in Gaul that this famous battle took place. Attila's forces consisted of the Gepid tribe, the Ostrogoths under Walamir, and the Huns under him. His forces were pitched against the Visigoths under Theodoric, ruler of southern Gaul; also, the Burgundians, Franks, and king Sangiban of the Alans under Aetius command who was able to muster an army of around 50,000 men.

Thorismund, Theodoric's son, was able to capture a small hill in the battle.

Because of this array of huge forces, Attila was defeated but did not give up his assaults.

In 452 C.E., he demanded the hand of Honoria, the sister of Valentinian III, the Western Roman Emperor, whom he wished to marry.

In order to force the marriage, he invaded the Italian peninsula. Valentinian tried to negotiate a peace treaty with Attila but, Attila refused his request.

His last resort was to engage Pope Leo I to negotiate for him. Attila and the Pope met at the Mincius River in northern Italy. Pope Leo I's words must have been very convincing as Attila left Italy.

This battle at Chalons has been one of significance for it kept Attila from dominating Western Europe.

Rome collapsed in 476 C.E. and, this victory over Attila's forces, helped to preserve the German culture which was to dominate Europe for a brief period.

The Catholic Church gained in importance at this time due to Pope Leo's popularity. It became, not only a staunch religious force, but also, a dominant political entity in Europe.

Its authority and power grew until it was challenged by Martin Luther in the 16th century.

Before Attila had the opportunity to invade Italy again, he died at the age of 47. His demise has been attributed to a bursting blood vessel on the night of his wedding to Hilda, a Gothic maiden.

His empire came to a close due to his sons' fighting among themselves over whom was to govern.

The Gepid tribe dealt the coup de grace to the Huns in 454 C.E.

The various subject tribes under their dominance rose up and fought for their independence which added another 'spike' to their downfall.

BYZANTINE EMPIRE

The Byzantine Empire developed out of the eastern half of the Roman Empire. At various times, the territories of the empire extended into the Balkans, Italy, North Africa, and Asia Minor, including the city of Rome.

In 395 C.E., this half of the Roman Empire was divided administratively which became a nightmare. In order to protect its borders, taxes were increased and bureaucrats were needed in order to raise the enormous amount of troops.

The emperor Diocletian, Constantine's predecessor, was the one who had split the empire into two parts, east and west, each with its own emperor, termed "Augustus" who had the assistance of a deputy and successor called "Caesar." This was done in order to facilitate the governing more pliable and easier.

Later, in 303 Diocletian persecuted the Christians, the so called Great Persecution. He ordered them to sacrifice to the gods or face torture, or death. The Christians didn't abide by this decree and died by the thousands.

Diocletian abdicated in 305 and his successor was his Caesar, Constantius who became Augustus of the Western Empire.

In 306, Constantius died while suppressing a rebellion in Britain where his son, Constantine, won support of his troops and became the new Augustus. However, his new position wasn't entirely accepted in Rome and it took him many years to develop a suitable reputation by campaigns to receive this honor.

In 312 C.E., his rival Maxentius, who was vying for the Western Empire, seized power in Rome while Constantine was engaged in battle in Gaul. Immediately, Constantine marched south to confront his adversary, Maxentius, at the Milvian Bridge.

While on this trek south, it has been recorded, that he saw a vision in the sky in the form of a cross bearing the inscription Hoc signo vinces, "in this sign you will conquer." Other stories say that he had a dream in which he saw Christ with the letters chi and rho that begins Christ's name in Greek.

Constantine then went ahead and had this monogram painted onto his soldiers' shields.

Maxentius plan to defeat Constantine at the bridge had backfired and he lost hundreds of his men who were swept down the river on boats; many had drowned in the water. Maxentius himself was drowned and his head was cut off, secured to a lance, and taken to Rome.

Because of this victory, Constantine now became the sole emperor of the Western Empire.

After the battle of Adrianople, Constantine embraced Christianity as a state religion. Before this time, the Christians were severely persecuted. Many were torched on the Appian Way. Also, they were thrown to the lions in the Coliseum for the entertainment of the Romans.

Despite all this mayhem, Christianity took root in the Middle East and spread to Egypt and Greece. Christian missionaries, such as Peter, the patriarch of Christianity, with his colleague, Saul of Tarsus (St. Paul), spread the word of the new faith to all parts of the Empire, including Rome.

As Christianity became very popular in Rome, it was perceived as a threat to unity, and therefore, the emperors began to persecute the Christians on a large scale.

The Christian church established its headquarters in Rome even though the Christians had to seek protection in the catacombs where they held their religious services.

As Christianity gained popularity, monasteries and religious communities were later found throughout the Byzantine Empire.

Constantine was able to solve a dispute between Arius, an Egyptian theologian priest who believed that Jesus was not God because he suffered and because God, not human, does not suffer and Athanasius who believed in the Catholic doctrine that Jesus was

God. At this time, Arius' belief was regarded as heretical and religious orthodoxy was given a definition so Christians knew what to believe. The Church, with the backing of the state, was able to resolve these theological disputes by legal means. At the Council of Nicaea in 325 which was called to rectify this problem, the Nicene Creed was drafted which set forth the basic Christian beliefs by which both sides, Arians and Catholics, could agree.

Constantine, by taking a step to solve religious problems, was able to make Christianity the dominant religion in Europe later on.

Constantine was born about 280 in a town call Naissus (present day Nis), in what is now Yugoslavia. His father was an officer in the army at one time and his son, Constantine spent much of his youth in Nicomedia where Emperor Diocletian's court was located.

Constantine, as stated, was the son of Constantius and became emperor after his father's demise.

Constantine had the old city of Byzantium rebuilt and renamed it Constantinople, his capital. He named it after himself. Today, this city is called Istanbul and has become one of the world's great cities. This city remained the capital of the Eastern Roman Empire until 1453 when the Ottoman Turks took over.

One of his early transactions was the Edict of Milan which stated that Christianity was a legal and tolerated religion. This Edict also stated that church property which had been confiscated during the period of persecution would be returned. Sunday was established as a day of worship.

Constantine's decrees gave the Church various immunities besides very useful privileges.

He has been noted for the construction of several basilicas—Church of the Nativity in Bethlehem and the Church of the Holy Sepulchre in Jerusalem.

His black mark was his persecution of the Jews. However, he did invoke civil legislation which was beneficial during his administration. For instance, he made a law which made certain occupations hereditary, namely bakers and butchers.

His decree concerning tenant farmers (coloni) didn't receive much acclaim as it forbade them to leave their land.

This and other legislation set the stage for the foundation of the entire social structure of medieval Europe.

It is interesting to note. Being a Christian, he chose not to be baptized until he was on his deathbed.

Despite his achievements in government, he has been regarded as a cruel, oppressive, and ruthless emperor. For instance, reasons unclear, in 326 C.E., he had his wife and eldest son put to death.

As always, all good things have to come to an end. Thus, it was with the reign of Constantine.

First of all, because of the extent of the regime, it took money to provide sufficient troops to guard its borders and this was a great strain on the finances of the empire. Second, the empire's economic trading business came into conflict with later Italian city-states, such as Venice and Genoa.

This came to a head during the fourth Crusade (1202-1204 C.E.) when the Venetians coerced crusading European knights to sack Constantinople.

After this plunder on the capital city of Constantinople (Istanbul), the Empire was weakened to such an extent that its walls were again breached by the invading army and cannons of the Ottoman Turks in 1453 C.E. This invasion has been regarded as the decline and destruction of a great empire.

As a final word, this empire was great enough to last for almost a millennium. This was due to several factors. One was its economy which was based on its agriculture a definite necessity if a nation is to survive. Second, because of its location on the narrow Bosporus Strait overlooking the Black Sea, it was at the crossroads for a vibrant trade between Asia and Europe which brought prosperity and wealth to its people.

Because of its economy, the arts and education flourished. Christian religion dominated the arts. The icons and mosaics depicted the saints, martyrs, and Jesus, his mother Mary, and the Apostles. One outstanding feature in writing was the illuminated manuscripts which showered the Bible.

In education, the empire's Orthodox Church should receive laurels for providing schools for parishes to train the laity and priests who taught a whole host of subjects—law, astronomy, grammar, music, philosophy, and medicine. Higher education wasn't to be outdone. In 850 C.E., the University of Constantinople trained lawyers and scholars for service in the imperial government. The literature of the empire centered on the salvation of the soul and encompassed obedience to God.

Byzantine's art, literature, and architecture was "contagious" for it was grasped by European scholars and Slavic and German peoples which, in turn, influenced their culture and traditions.

The legacy of the Byzantium Empire has to be the spread of the Christian religion which has endured to the present time throughout the world.

A

B

Black, Jeremy. Professor. <u>Encyclopedia of World History</u>. London, Dempsey Parr Book, 2000

Boyle, David and others. <u>History Makers</u>. Bath, U.K. Parragon Publishing Book, 20005

Brown, Reference Group <u>World History</u>. London, U.K. Sandcastle Books Ltd., 2008

C

Caldwell, Wallace E. <u>The New Popular History of the World</u>. Vol. One. The Greystone Press, 1964

Cantor, Norman F. <u>The Civilization of the Middle Ages</u>. N.Y. Harper Collins Publishers, Inc. 1993

D

Davison, Michael Worth. <u>When, Where, Why and How It Happened</u>.
London, The Reader's Digest Association, 1993.

E

F

G

Greer, Michele and Staff. <u>National Geographic Essential Visual History of the World</u>. Washington, D.C. National Geographic Society, 2007

H

Hall, Timothy C. The Complete Idiot's Guide to World History. N.Y. Penquin Group, 2008

Hart, Michael H. The 100. N.Y. Carol Publishing Group Edition, 1995

Hitchcock, Liz Editor. The Truth About History. London, Planet Three Publishing Network, 2007

Hurdman, Charlotte, Steele, Philip, James, Richard. The encyclopedia of the Ancient World. Beth, U.K. Southwater Publisher, 2000

I

J

K

L

Lanning, Michael Lee. Lt. Col. (Ret.). <u>The Military 100</u>. N.Y. Barnes and Nobles, 1996

Lewis, Brenda Ralph. <u>Great Civilizations</u>. Bath, U.K. 1999

M

Mackay, Dr. James. <u>World Facts</u>. Bath, U.K. Parragon Publishing book, 1999

Morgan, David. <u>The Mongols</u>. Oxford, U.K. Blackwell Publishers, 1987

N

Nelson, Rebecca, Editor. <u>The Handy History Answer Book</u>. N.Y. Barnes and Noble Books, 1999

Noorden, Djinn, Pickering, David. <u>History of the World</u>. N.Y. Dorling Kindersley, 1994

O

P

Q

R

Roberts, G.M. A <u>Concise History of the World</u>. N.Y. Oxford University Press, Inc., 1995

S

Stuart, Gene S. <u>The Mighty Aztecs</u>. Washington, D.C. National Geographic Society, 1981

T

U

V

W

Wells, H.G. <u>An Illustrated Short History of the World</u>. London, Webb and Bower, 1987

White, J.E. Manchip. <u>Ancient History its Culture and History</u>. N.Y. Dover Publications, Inc., 1970

Whittemore, Walter, J. <u>World Battles and Their Leaders Who Changed Global History</u>. Iuniverse Publisher, Bloomington, Indiana, 2008

X

Y

Yenna, Bill. <u>100 Events That Shaped World History</u>. San Mateo, CA. Blue Books, 1993

Z

ABOUT THE AUTHOR

Walter graduated from San Diego State University in 1950 and holds a Bachelor of Arts degree. He majored in Physical Education and minored in Social Studies. He received a general secondary credential, a Master of Arts degree and an administrative credential from the same institution.

He had taught in the public schools of California for the past thirty years and is now retired. During this period of time, he taught various subjects but, mainly, fixed his attention on American and World History.

When he retired, he became very interested in umpiring and refereeing various sports, such as, baseball, softball, basketball, football and volleyball on a high school and college level.

He received a certificate of merit from the National Softball Association held at Burbank, California, also, at the Regional Umpire School at Pleasantville, California. He attended and received his professional umpire certificate at Harry Wendelstad's Umpire School in 1985 at Daytona Beach, Florida. Because of a bad back, he was forced to retire after fifteen years of umpiring.

He served as a hospital corpsman with the 4th Marine Division during WWII from 1943 to 1945 and took part in the battles of Saipan, Tinian and Iwo Jima where he was nearly killed by an explosive shell which heaved him into the air.

At age of eighty-eight he decided to engage in writing which he enjoys immensely.